RATHER DUMB

A Top Tabloid Reporter
Tells CBS
How to Do News

Mike Walker

NELSON CURRENT

A Division of Thomas Nelson, Inc.

Published in Nashville, Tennessee, by Nelson Current, a division of a wholly-owned subsidiary (Nelson Communications, Inc.) of Thomas Nelson, Inc.

Nelson Current books may be purchased in bulk for educational, business, fundraising, or sales promotional use. For information, please email SpecialMarkets@ThomasNelson.com.

Library of Congress Cataloging-in-Publication Data
Walker, Mike (Brian E.)
   Rather dumb : a top tabloid reporter tells CBS how to do news / Mike Walker.
      p. cm.
Includes Index.
ISBN 1-5955-5018-6
1. Press and politics—United States—History—20th century. 2. Television broadcasting of news—United States. 3. Presidents—United States—Election 2004. 4. Rather, Dan. I. Title.
   PN4888.P6W26   2005
   070.4'3—dc22   2004030535

Printed in the United States of America
05 06 07 08 09   QKP   5 4 3 2 1

To my family, who reap the whirlwind and smile in the face of it. Thanks to Enquirer *colleague Deborah Hughes, sharp-penciled editor Joel Miller, my just-plain-sharp agent Dan Strone, publisher David Dunham—and the inimitable Brunhilde Frappe. Tip of the hat to fascinating website Ratherbiased.com, which, sadly, now follows its subject into retirement.*

Contents

"If a rooster squawks, don't be too quick to strangle him. He might be trying to tell you something."

—DAN RATHER (?)

Preface

Whenever I begin a book about a breaking news story—this is my fourth—I face two problems: how to deal with information that breaks during the writing and hoping that the book won't be rendered invalid by events which occur after we go to press. My books about the O.J. Simpson trial, for instance, were published before the final verdict, but both were still-relevant bestsellers.

This time out, I have simply interrupted narrative to comment on each new Rathergate break as it occurred. But—*déja vu!*—as this book goes to press, "defendant" Dan Rather, like the O.J. of yore, still awaits a final verdict from so-called independent experts hired by CBS. Their mission: to investigate how the CBS News journalism process produced a lie about President George Bush that was compounded by endless stonewalling and name-calling at all who dared question it.

CBS moguls had promised the report "in a few weeks." But as of this writing, three *months* have passed—and still no verdict. Rumors drifting out of CBS had hinted that the independent panel's report would be greatly delayed, even that parts of it might never be made public. If true, that would constitute another ill-conceived move by CBS News, making it even more difficult to rehabilitate its credibility.

But I predict that by the time you hold this book in your

hands, dear reader, you will know what we did not—the final judgment of the CBS-hired panel. And that actually will make this book an even more interesting exercise. Now you can compare the panel's judgment with your own. So join our Jury as we proceed with The Trial of Dan Rather. You will hear relevant evidence clearly presented by this Court. You will be shown real-life examples of what constitutes solid journalistic procedure. After due deliberation, you will make up your own mind about super-anchor Dan Rather's journalistic guilt or innocence. So put aside any so-called "independent" verdict, *compadres!* I've got news for you:

We don' need no steeenking verdict!

The only verdict that matters is . . . yours. Here is where you, The Jury, will render history's judgment on Dan Rather after Hizzoner, The Judge (yours truly), guides you through the bizarre twists and turns of a riveting case that marks a watershed moment in American journalism.

One more thing: my opinions are my own and do not necessarily reflect those of my paper, the *National Enquirer*.

All rise, please . . . the Court is now in session!

Chapter 1

This story is true! . . . With respect, answer the questions."
It was vintage Dan Rather.

Sitting for an interview with the *New York Observer*, the mighty anchorman/aristocrat shrugged off the media hellfire raining on his CBS News empire, bared his teeth at the White House, and stubbornly defended the dumb-ass George W. Bush/National Guard "documents" story, which had been shot down so swiftly by mainstream media and Internet bloggers just hours after he broke it on national TV.

He'd endured a week of scorn from all quarters—including document experts and a snippy First Lady, Laura Bush, who used the word "forgeries." Now the famously thin-skinned news star had had enough. Hotter than a rooster on Viagra, as he might put it in that *faux* Texas speak he so adores, Dan looked—as he often does—ready to open fire on a crowded mall as he hurled his defiant challenge at the president of the United States:

"With respect, answer the questions."

It was one good ol' Texas boy telling another: Dubya, answer my questions, even though these National Guard documents might be phony—because my story needs some credibility. Y'all come clean now, dammit!

Quite a ballsy ploy. Like most journalists, I admire cheeky newsboy *chutzpah* as immortalized by brash reporter Hildy Johnson in *The Front Page*. Now here was Dan Rather, CBS TV icon and major player in the Media Elite, pulling a stunt so bizarre it made you wonder, just for a moment, if he was employing some sophisticated secret technique known only to newsdom's top tier. But, no! Dan was simply—brazenly—tossing a Hail Mary pass, blatantly obfuscating the issue by implying that even if the documents that cast major aspersions on the president's military record were fake, the story itself was true.

Dan's concept was breathtaking, vaguely McLuhanesque. Was he seriously positing that the medium is not the message, after all?

Hell, no! Dogg just be shuckin' and jivin' 'cause he knows he's busted!

It was as if I, mongering along in my humble news niche as gossip editor of the *National Enquirer*, had, after slapdash attempts at authentication, published in my column scandalous documents about a major celebrity, only to have them exposed as amateurish forgeries. Just for fun, let's say my bogus papers revealed, in lurid detail, that comedian Jimmy Fallon of *Saturday Night Live* fame was a serial molester of Catholic priests, and that this rogue ex-altar boy had inflicted an STD on a certain Father O'Reilly.

Now, I'm no Dan Rather. But as a newsman who's battled my way to borderline fame, or notoriety, if you will—millions read my signed column and see my face above it—I'm desperate to maintain my hard-earned reputation for accuracy. I know that once a celebrity sin is confessed and the gory details chewed over, people quickly get bored. Were I caught in such a scandal, I'd take the course of action that always, always works: I'd admit the screw up, beg the mercy of my readers with misty eyes, and apologize abjectly to the usually good-natured Mr. Fallon.

Apparently, however, that is not how it is done by the Media Elite (as opposed to the media Big Leagues, of which I actually am a member because of the *Enquirer*'s huge circulation). I can't tell you what's advised in the CBS Handbook for TV Journalists—if there is such a thing—but based on the early evidence, the approved network technique for handling a pesky caught-with-your-pants-down débacle is deny, deny, deny! Attack all questioners as "partisan ideologues"! Go on the offensive!

Phony documents? Hey, no problemo! Simply concede that they might be a tad flaky, then get terminally aggressive. Immediately demand a full and frank interview from the victim—on the grounds that even though the documents may be bogus, the story is true and you insist on, with respect, an answer to all your questions.

Wow! So that's how it's done in the Media Elite. Hildy Johnson would be impressed. I certainly am. As a modest tabloid toiler, I've slogged along for years breaking stories the hard way—cultivating reliable contacts in places where news is likely to happen, developing sources who trust me with valuable info that might even lead to a No. 1 *New York Times* bestseller—like my book on the O. J. Simpson trial. So, I'm actually embarrassed to admit I've never had the genius to ply the phony document dodge.

Using Dan Rather's technique, I could, er, "discover" a phony birth certificate that says Angelina Jolie is actually a man! Then, following the CBS template, I'd trumpet the documents in my column, wait for them to be discredited by experts—then challenge Angelina in a column headlined: "This story is true! With respect, *disrobe.*"

Now there's a fantasy. But as news technique, it's . . . Rather dumb!

Lest you think I'm misrepresenting the Darth Vader of network news, I'll let him explain the elitist theory of phony document denial in his own words:

> I think the public, even decent people who are well-disposed toward President Bush, understand that powerful and extremely well-financed forces are focusing on questions about the documents because they can't deny the fundamental truth of the story. If you can't deny the information, then attack and seek to destroy the credibility of the messenger, the bearer of the information. And in this case, it's change the subject from the truth of the information to the truth of the documents.

Vintage Dan blather!

He avers in the above that "powerful and extremely well-financed forces are focusing on questions about the documents!"

That's right, Dan. Those "forces" are otherwise known as "the press!" It's us, your colleagues! And here are the questions we're focusing on:

- Why were you willing to accept the word of an avowed Bush hater?

- Why didn't you verify the origin of a document that wasn't even an original, but a copy?
- Who forged the documents?
- Why did you rush to foist a smear of a sitting president's military record just fifty days before a presidential election without triple-checking your facts?
- And why, when the press asked legitimate questions about your story, did you look into the camera and voice the outrageous lie that it was only "partisan political ideological forces" that raised such doubts?

Enquiring minds want to know, Dan.

I want to know.

With respect, answer the questions.

Have you no shame, sir? Are you finally so arrogant, so inflated by your legendary ego that you refuse to consider the idea that perhaps it's time you were floated out to sea on the next ice floe? Did you not consider that scary scenario when you turned seventy-three this past Halloween? As an objective, balanced journalist, don't you agree it's time you were gently shown the door?

The *New York Post* asked the embattled anchorman that question. He replied, "I don't have a date [to retire]. I don't have a timetable. As long as I like doing it, as long as I think I can do it at least reasonably well—and, most importantly, as long as the people I work for think that I can do it reasonably well, then I want to continue doing it. I have a passion for what I do. I love what I do."

Can Dan survive? On the Internet, enraged bloggers blogged: THROW THIS ANCHOR OVERBOARD!

His CBS News anchor/managing editor predecessor, the respected Walter Cronkite, said publicly he would have fired Dan Rather years ago, after he stormed out of the CBS newsroom in a raging temper and left the network dark for six long minutes—an eternity in TV time.

And Rathergate? As they say in TV, folks, "Join me for an exclusive, in-depth probe of the document debacle, coming up next! *You* sit in the jury box as we conduct the Trial of Dan Rather."

But first, as I mentioned in the Preface, let me point out that as I write this book about Rathergate—an ongoing media cause célèbre—there is breaking news about the case I will deal with as it happens. So far, the CBS-ordered independent investigation of the boondoggle is not complete. Not that it matters to us. Because who—outside of CBS—needs it? We already know enough facts to judge Dan Rather's conduct. Barring a heretofore-unknown murder or other odd twist, the story is ripe to be told, so I'm going to tell it. And how am I qualified to sit in judgment? Well, like many reporters who rose to be editors, I've sat in on the postmortems of story screw-ups—either as a potential suspect or as editor-in-charge of the inquisition. Trust me when I tell you: An unbiased first look at facts already in evidence clearly indicates that Dan & Company committed mind-blowing gaffes of journalistic judgment and simple common sense. Whatever the CBS investigation uncovers will be fine print, believe me, unless . . . unless Dan's producer, Mary Mapes, testifies that her boss Dan ordered her to

contact presidential candidate John Kerry's campaign to tip them about the Bush-bashing documents! That would be a bombshell. The story would escalate from Rather Dumb to . . . Rather Biased!

But that's not going to happen. I believe Dan Rather is a strident liberal guilty of bias in the news he presents and in the way he presents it. Do I believe his driving motive here was to torpedo Bush's campaign? No! Would he love to see Bush embarrassed and defeated? Yes! But . . . .

As a veteran reporter, let me suggest that Mary Mapes put her source—Texas Bush hater Bill Burkett—in touch with the Kerry camp simply to keep him happy and get her paws on those documents. It wouldn't be the first time a reporter cut a corner to cut a deal—it won't be the last. And Mapes, as you'll learn in the pages ahead, has a history of improperly currying favor with sources to get what she wants.

So, let's reel our minds back to that original breathless broadcast on September 8, 2004, when CBS anchorman Dan Rather reported his exclusive discovery of Texas National Guard documents and presented them as proof that (1) George Bush was a lazy no-show during his military service, (2) he was grounded as a pilot because he ducked his mandatory medical exam, and (3) he got kid-glove treatment from a superior officer because of pressure from his daddy's powerful friends.

The report made major headlines after it aired on *60 Minutes II*, the Wednesday night clone of the venerable and respected *60 Minutes*. A veteran of the long-running original, Morley Safer, condemned the report and sent a cannonball screaming across Dan Rather's bow in a *New York Times* interview.

"These are not standards that would have been tolerated, and it's inconceivable this would have made it on the air on the Sunday show," Safer snapped.

Adding to Rather's embarrassment was a report on the Internet site *The Washington Note* that *Fahrenheit 9/11* director Michael Moore said in a speech at the University of Central Arkansas that he'd been offered the fraudulent documents from the same CBS source while making his movie, but he turned them down. If true, that's an eyeopener. Moore, a rabid liberal partisan under no journalistic constraints, *didn't* trust the documents or their source—but Dan Rather *did?*

Consider this: While grilling veteran *60 Minutes* gasbag/commentator Andy Rooney, radio talk-show host Don Imus was incredulous that CBS News had so casually accepted anti-Bush activist Bill Burkett—an ex-National Guard malcontent with admitted mental problems—as a source of "unimpeachable" integrity, to use Dan Rather's word.

Imus told Rooney: "The first thing we would have done, if we had been contacted by Burkett, we would've Googled him . . . if you Google the guy, you come up with what looks like somebody . . . who has an over-the-top agenda."

It's an ironclad rule of journalism, and it's plain old common sense: Before you deal with a source, know exactly who they are.

Interestingly, Andy Rooney—as he often does—then blurted an opinion that undoubtedly made his bosses wince, hinting at a question that's plagued CBS for years: Shouldn't Dan have been dumped because he's just plain weird, a loose cannon who might someday blow up the whole blasted ship? Rooney said:

"[Dan] gives the impression of falseness sometimes that does not exist in his character. I think he is a first-class guy, a good guy and an honest guy. And yet, there is something about the way he behaves sometimes that makes people suspicious of him. And it's too bad."

Too bad, perhaps, but when you're a TV anchor, perception is reality. Rathergate aside, why didn't CBS deep-six their anchor years ago after his sinking ratings dragged their evening news down to dead-last behind NBC's Tom Brokaw and ABC's Peter Jennings? It's hard to believe CBS execs know nothing of that jumpy unease so many viewers experience when they stare into Rather's piercing, pugnacious eyes and sense the volcano bubbling inside. News business insiders have always puzzled about the network's almost saintly tolerance of that edgy alter ego known as. . . .

Dan, Dan, The Loony Man.

To quote Imus again: "Watching Dan Rather do the news, he looks like he's making a hostage tape. They should have guys in ski masks and AK-47s just standing off to the side."

Even Dan's ardent attempts to be a warm, folksy guy were often off-putting. Remember the lame *My Three Sons* sweaters he wore for a while? And how one night he suddenly looked us in the eyes and signed off—just for a week, actually, until execs muzzled him—with that one word: "Courage"?

And who has not marveled at his wacko Texasisms or Ratherisms, as they're sometimes called? The whole country buzzed that Dan's screws were loosening visibly when he babbled on election night 2000: "Sip it, savor it, cup it, Photostat it, underline it in red, put it in the album, hang it on the wall, George Bush is the next president of the United States."

But Dan has survived ongoing suspicions of lunacy for decades, so let's get back to the burning question: Should he be bounced for Rathergate? To restate the case: If he truly believed that the documents proved George W. Bush shirked his duty in the Texas National Guard, despite bright-red flags warning that they might be phony, CBS News team leader Dan was demonstrably incompetent. And if he knew there was a strong possibility that they were phony, yet still rushed to "break" the story, he's almost certainly guilty of political bias and trying to influence a presidential election just fifty days away.

Keep two facts firmly in mind when judging Dan: On CBS News, he's not just another "talking head" who reads teleprompter copy written by others. Or so he tells us—endlessly. Dan proudly asserts he's a guy who hits the street and reports the news. Hands on. Lotsa elbow grease. But more than that, he's the managing editor—a title he fought for like a pit bull on PCP, right, Tex? Managing editor is not, as Dan constantly reminds us, an honorary title. It is a major position of authority. It means that Dan is the big dog and deserves the heat when his team screws up. Yet he's told the *New York Post* and others—even before the independent investigators began their work—that he has no plans to retire. And, he says, he sure as hell won't resign.

With respect, folks, answer the question. Should Dan Rather have been fired? (At this point, we know he's retiring from the anchor chair, though the plan is for him to stay on as a reporter for both versions of *60 Minutes*—returning to the scene of the crime, so to speak.)

Me, I'm not so sure—not that Dan gives a damn what a newsman from the *National Enquirer* thinks. Ah ain't one of them Media Elites, y'all! But I hesitate to demand he should be drummed out of his job because (1) I'm naturally cautious about dissing anybody who's got Dan's scary look *and* was born on Halloween, and (2) I get jumpy as a frog on a campfire skillet (feel free to grab that, Dan . . . if you haven't already) when it comes to jeering a rival journo who blows a story. It's an occupational fear, believe me. If there's one refrain you keep reading about and hearing from journalists as we pick over Dan's bones, it's "There but for the grace of God go I."

Trust me: There isn't a good journalist alive who's never been wrong. It's so easy to get sloppy on fact-checking and oh so tempting to believe a story you desperately want to believe—one you just feel deep down in your gut is true. But journalists are haunted by the knowledge that even when you do everything right, even after you shine relentless, cynical light down every rat hole, something slimy still can slither up and bite your ass.

Over a lifetime in the news business—working for wire services, daily newspapers, TV, radio, and the world's most feared and famous tabloid—I've composed prissy homilies about the business of newsgathering to which my reporters are forced to listen endlessly. Here's one to stitch on your sampler:

Every time you publish a story, you're jumping off a cliff . . .
so hope it's a bungee jump.

Dan crashed and hit bottom. He's alive and in a lot of pain, but the question that rivets both fans and detractors is: Should he be allowed to survive? Before I get to the end of these musings and a step-by-step postmortem, I'll know the answer to that question.

And so will you, dear reader. So will you.

If you're an instant-gratification freak, you can jump ahead to Chapter 9 and my Rathergate Timeline—the day-by-day breakdown of what CBS knew, when they knew it, and when they knew they didn't know a damn thing. But I urge you to hang on and take the journey. Be patient. Be meticulous. Examine the background and the players. Good investigative reporters insist on thorough background research—even when they're on deadline—before rushing a breaking news story into print or onto the airwaves. Perhaps Dan Rather was preaching a similar sermon of caution to reporters tempted to impetuousness when he disgorged himself of this pithy wisdom: "Even Uncle Charlie sometimes cuts firewood with a dull blade."

Then again, who the hell knows what Dan means when he's in Yoda-from-Texas mode?

Why dwell on Rathergate? Is it, finally, nothing more than a tempest in journalism's teapot? Folks, don't you believe it! Keeping the press honest is crucial, now as never before. Well-informed Americans know it's not melodramatic to warn that we're suddenly in an age when dark and powerful forces are assaulting freedom of the press. George W. Bush and his attorney general wield the Patriot Act to thwart journalists exercising our First Amendment right to investigate government's innermost workings—just as our Founding Fathers intended when we escaped that other King George. As this is written, reporters from the *New York Times* and *Time* magazine are threatened with jail because someone in Bush's inner circle committed a crime and blew the cover of an undercover CIA agent to columnist Robert Novak, who's forever shamed because he published a name no one needed to know. And will somebody please explain why the pompous Novak's not threatened with jail? (Can you say "right-wing Bushie sellout," children?)

Never doubt that press-hating ideologues giggle like teenyboppers as poll after poll shows that more and more Americans distrust the media. And who can blame them? But here's the danger, you media haters: Someday, you might need the free press when the cops, or the courts, or the federal government won't listen to your pleas for simple justice. We ain't much, but we're damn handy when you need us. Who said it better than Rather himself when, many years ago, he was protesting massive layoffs of news staff at CBS?

"Journalism . . . is a light on the horizon. A beacon that helps citizens of a democracy find their way."

Well said, Dan. Trouble is, when lying clowns like so-called "reporters" Jayson Blair and Jack Kelley stain the integrity of the *New York Times* and *USA Today,* or when CNN and Time magazine are forced to admit the inaccuracy of a joint report that the U.S. military used nerve gas on Vietnam defectors, it opens the door for corrupt powerbrokers to denigrate the press as untrustworthy and to deny the wrongdoings we expose. So if Dan Rather, the face of CBS News, rushes onto the air with an explosive scandal about a sitting president that's based on reportage abysmally below professional standards, the power of the press—which protects you when no one else will, Mr. and Ms. America—is dangerously weakened.

Know this: Rathergate, *no matter how it plays out,* is a major event.

Tom Rosenstiel, director of the Project for Excellence in Journalism, laid it down hard when he said Rather's story, based on sloppy reporting and fake documents, is "the end of the era of network news."

There's an old bromide that one of the surest indicators a story's truly huge is when TV's late-night comedians start cracking jokes about it. On NBC's *Tonight* show, it was hardly a surprise that Jay Leno joked about the controversy boiling around rival CBS's star anchor. But what a shocker it must have been for Rather—and his CBS News boss, Andrew Heyward—when their network's own comedy star, David Letterman, turned the controversy into a punch line!

In an astounding skewering many in the media swear is unprecedented, CBS funmeister Letterman shoved it right up the wazoo of his homeboy Dan *and* the network news division, after they finally quit their despicable stonewalling and admitted they'd blown it. Interestingly—for me, anyway—Dave's scathing comedy drive-by "borrowed" from a bit I created eight years ago on the *Howard Stern Show.* I have performed it nearly every Friday morning since. It's called "The Mike Walker Gossip Game." Stern introduces it something like this:

"Okay, here's Mike Walker from the *National Enquirer . . .* a paper I love because it's always packed with stories I want to read. I have to say that or Mike will report me in bed with a guy! Here's how we play the game. Mike tells us four stories. Three are true and will be in his column next week, but one is a fake he's concocted to fool us. So we have to pick which is the phony gossip news."

Millions of Howard's fans, and my circle of news colleagues and pals, are familiar with the bit. That's why my phone started ringing off the hook late on Monday, September 20— and well into the next day—after Letterman did his hilarious take on the just-breaking news that Dan Rather and CBS News President Andrew Heyward had admitted they'd been duped by the phony George W. Bush National Guard "documents."

Inspired by the idea of trying to identify fake news, Letterman set up the bit in his *Late Show* opening monologue by commenting on the Dan Rather/CBS News controversy, then he picked it up with bandleader Paul Shafer. Here's the transcript:

DAVE: Ohmigod, you folks been following the big scandal going on here at CBS? CBS News . . . you know what I'm talking about? It's pretty nasty. And the memos about President Bush and the National Guard? And CBS is now saying . . . "Hey, it's not us, we were misled, we're the victims of a colossal hoax." . . . Incidentally, that's the same thing they said after hiring me.

PAUL: Oh!

(APPLAUSE)

DAVE: . . . that CBS News controversy—we were talking

about this a minute ago—is not going away. It's just not
going away. You know what I'm talking about?

PAUL: Yeah, I've been reading about it.

DAVE: Look now at what they're doing.

(Taped intro for CBS News)

ANNOUNCER: Tonight on the *CBS Evening News,* we
report nine real stories and one fake one. Can you guess
which is which? You may be surprised. Only on the *CBS
Evening News.*

(APPLAUSE)

DAVE: You may be surprised.

PAUL: I will be surprised.

It's always a surprise when you're mugged in your own
neighborhood. But hand it to Dave for teaching the network
"weasels," as he calls his bosses, the lesson they never seem to
learn: The best way to handle a screw-up is head-on, with a
dollop of humor to defuse the tension. That's exactly what
Dan Rather and CBS initially refused to do, treating the
nation once again to the tortured dance of stiff, arrogant
apparatchiks *a la* Nixon who never anticipate the horror that
invariably ensues when mistakes aren't dealt with swiftly and
forthrightly. Here's the rule, and it's not just for journalists:

The coverup is always worse than the crime.

Hey . . . Media Elite! Don't you ever learn?

Pay attention, mainstream screw-ups. Yes, you—*New York
Times, USA Today, Washington Post, 60 Minutes,* CBS News,

Los Angeles Times, CNN and *Time* magazine, NBC News, *Boston Globe,* etc. It's time for a trip to the woodshed, a painful refresher course in hard-knuckle, common-sense journalism—of the kind practiced by, say, the *National Enquirer.*

Here's Lesson No. 1: *Lose your hubris!*

Incredibly, *hubris* isn't considered a dirty word in the Media Elite dictionary—but it should be. Arrogance and exaggerated pride are dangerous attitudes that can strike newsmen blind at crucial moments. Case in point: our own Dan Rather, the pompous, pugnacious reporter who rocketed to national notoriety for preying on Republican presidents. Dan kicked his career into hyper-drive with his public savaging of Richard Nixon in 1974. Attack dog tactics made him a media star. But dogs who turn rabid tend to lunge blindly. Dan's George W. Bush/National Guard "exclusive" missed its mark because it had no teeth. A sad coda to the career of an old newshound, who stands warily at bay as the media critics howl: Put him down!

Oh, Danny Boy . . . the pipes, the pipes are calling. . . .

Chapter 2

Who is Dan Rather?

Test your anchor IQ by identifying this phrase: "What's the frequency, Kenneth?"

Does it refer to:

(A) An off-Broadway play highly acclaimed by critics?

(B) The title of a song by rock band REM, which had its TV debut on David Letterman's *Late Show*?

(C) The utterance of a berserk weirdo as he kicked the crap out of Dan on a New York street?

Answer: All of the above!

So, who is Dan Rather? Obvious answer: One of network television's Three Wise Men—the legendary anchors of the six o'clock evening news—Tom Brokaw on NBC, Peter Jennings on ABC, Dan Rather on CBS. But our cowboy's much, much more than that.

Just compare Daring Dan's thunder-and-lightning career to that of bland Brokaw or the jejune Jennings. Marvel at the enjambment of the sober-sided newsman melding seamlessly with the edgy, ironic weirdo, and what you get is that offbeat cat who eyeballs the camera and coolly announces on Election Night 1996: "This race . . . is hot and tight as a too-small bathing suit on a too-long car ride back from the beach!" (We'll deal with Dan's "ad lib" Danisms later, but note for now that he repeated nearly the exact phrase on Election Night 2000.)

Thumb this zeitgeist trivia into your Blackberry, kids: Dan Rather is a bona fide American pop culture idol!

Count the number of times you've seen him lampooned on TV shows, from *Saturday Night Live* to the *Late Show.* Comedians and talk show hosts around the radio and TV dial, as well as newspaper and magazine writers gleefully quote his bizarre Texasisms:

"If a frog had side pockets, he'd carry a handgun."

"He's the kind of a guy who would fight a rattlesnake—and give the snake a two-bite start."

"Democrats and Republicans are nervous as pigs in a packing plant over these returns."

"Bush is sweeping through the South like a tornado through a trailer park."

As Larry King once told him, "Dan, you sound like the newsman's Ross Perot!"

Dan Rather—a pop culture icon? As the Brits would put it, "Rah-*ther!*" Consider the new stanza added to the Ballad of Dan Rather in the year 2000, when he was immortalized in yet another rock-and-roll anthem. And this time, he was listed as co-artist on the sensationally titled "Rocked By Rape!"

This pointed parody—a critique of violence in network news—was the co-production of a San Francisco-based record company and a band called Evolution Control Committee. The song is composed of phrases spoken by Dan on CBS newscasts, edited over music samples from AC/DC's song "Black In Black."

Once again, Dan was spinning in the zeitgeist after a provocative review by the influential music mag *Spin,* which raved that the artists "plunge the knife hilariously deep into anchor/stiff Dan Rather. Notorious for writing his own crude rhymes, the CBS hairpiece intones about 'fraudulent drug thugs' and 'hidden Nazis next door' and the ECC splice it all into a wicked language poem, backed by an endless AC/DC drone."

Cool! The ECC rockers got a nasty letter from CBS lawyers that began: "A matter of serious concern has come to our attention!" It blathered on and on about how use of Dan's voice "significantly infringes on the copyright by CBS. We hereby advise you. . . ." Blah, blah, blah. ECC wrote back to inform CBS lawyers that "copyright law itself allows for people to make 'fair use' of copyrighted materials for purposes of parody. 'Rocked By Rape' is *nothing* if not parody."

Right on, bro! CBS garnered nothing from their efforts to stomp out the obscure rock record. But the ensuing publicity ignited interest and radio airplay for the catchy ditty. ECC, wary of fighting a legal battle against giant CBS, stopped pressing new copies of the single, but made it available on their CD *Plagiarhythm Nation.*

"Rocked By Rape" is an authentic poem. It's based on phrases written and spoken by Dan Rather, and has three verses and a chorus. The first verse goes like this:

this is the cbs evening news
with dan rather reporting from
cbs news headquarters in new york
good evening

danger war killer fraud
cia mayhem crisis horrible
inflation military threat
flaming debris fatal heart attack
stress injuries prison disaster
economic collapse dangerous radiation
a tide of violence and human misery
a liar and an unremorseful killer
communist international smuggling pipeline
starving victims and how they died
chemical weapons carpet bomb death
tough fbi killed and injured children
police conspiracy negative attacks
discipline sex and drinking binges
dying of a heart attack dying of breast cancer
dying of a Japanese nuclear bomb
mountains of credit card debt
a mountain of cocaine tons of cocaine
atomic bomb radiation experiments
unwitting test subjects dangerous radiation
marijuana abuse hooked on drugs
time for us to bug out
rocked rocked rocked by rape
rocked rocked rocked by rape
rocked rocked rocked by rape
sex drugs and rocked by rape

Pithy poetry, indeed. Rather has never commented on this
interesting artistic venture. One hopes he'd be both amused

and bemused. Or perhaps he'd simply like to kick the crap out of these long-haired punks!

"What's the frequency, Kenneth?"

With respect, answer the question: Who *is* Dan Rather?

The brash, ballsy son of roughneck dad Irvin "Rags" Rather, who made his living digging ditches in the dusty Texas oil fields, Dan Rather was a rags-to-riches kid in the classic mold. He started working in professional journalism even before he graduated college, taking on "stringer" assignments from the Associated Press, United Press International and local radio stations. He met a young woman named Jean, who worked at a radio station, and they married. Working at a Houston TV station in 1961, he impressed his bosses when he chained himself to a tree and reported live from the heart of Hurricane Carla. "We were impressed by his physical courage," said Walter Cronkite. "He was ass deep in water moccasins."

In 1962, Rather was hired as a correspondent for CBS News and, as he explains in his autobiography *The Camera Never Blinks*, he became—quite by accident, almost—the first reporter to phone in the news that President John F. Kennedy had been assassinated.

Sometimes, that's all it takes to catapult you onto journalism's fast track—one lucky break. It's amazing how often being the first reporter to pick up a ringing telephone in a busy newsroom will land you on the front page or on TV's evening news.

Rather's phone call came shortly after his promotion to the post of CBS bureau chief in New Orleans. Network bosses ordered him to set up coverage for President John F.

Kennedy's precampaign swing through Dallas. "My first reaction was one of irritation," he recalled. "I was still struggling to get the bureau organized. The civil rights movement was exploding all around us. Now this."

So days later, Rather stood on a Dallas street near the infamous grassy knoll as JFK's motorcade came into view. "Suddenly, I was aware that a police car had passed me, taking the wrong turnoff, going like hell," said Rather. Craning his neck, he saw the presidential limousine whip past, but he could not see the president. He thought he'd spotted Mrs. Kennedy, but it was all a blur as the motorcade roared past.

"I had not heard a shot. I was only vaguely aware of the hustle and bustle and noise and confusion taking place somewhere behind me. None of the scene came with any precision. Something had happened. But what?"

Rather hot-footed it five blocks back to TV station KRLD. Running inside to the news desk, he yelled at staffers to turn state and local police radios on full blast. Instantly, it was clear something big had gone down. The radio chatter was intense. Cops were heard asking each other what the hell was going on. Rather caught a reference to Parkland Hospital, looked up the number, and dialed. Right away he lucked out. A frazzled hospital operator admitted, "The president has been shot. I don't know anything else."

Rather begged the operator to put a doctor on. She did, and he confirmed JFK had been shot. He added it was "his understanding" that the president was dead, but he refused to give his name and hung up. Not enough. Not confirmation. Rather dialed the switchboard again and asked to speak to anyone in authority. The rattled, impatient operator told him everything was in great confusion, that all the doctors were busy. Recalled Rather:

"There was a pause, then she lowered her voice and said, 'Two Catholic fathers are standing here in the hall.' I said, 'Would you ask one of the priests if I might speak to him?'"

The priest came on the line and admitted the president was dead. Rather asked if he was sure. "Yes, unfortunately, I am," said the priest—and hung up. Rather quickly told the local news director what he had. Moments later, he got a shock when he heard a voice from CBS in New York announce to the local radio desk: "Rather says the president is dead."

He recalls how hearing that bulletin for which only he was responsible gave him "a chill. It dawned on me it was possible I had committed a blunder beyond comprehension, beyond forgiving. . . . If I had been given two seconds to think about it . . . I would have said, whoa, better run that past someone else."

It was the perfect illustration of that little mantra mentioned earlier, the one I repeat to myself just before I sign off on a story: *Every time you publish, you're jumping off a cliff . . . so hope it's a bungee jump.*

Think about this: Reporters are almost *never* eyewitness to any event. We're ambulance chasers, if you will, always arriving after the accident or incident. Our job is to keep cool, ask questions skillfully, and not be influenced by the emotions that surge around news events. You gather facts, check and recheck, then cross your fingers and pray when your editor yells, "We're on deadline, dammit! What have you got?" If you haven't got it, you've got to have the balls to say, "It won't fly."

Your editor won't be thrilled, but he'll get over it. Because the one thing that's worse than missing the story is getting it wrong, as Dan Rather did when he blew open the barn doors on those scandalous documents that could have affected the presidential election—and then discovered he'd been duped.

Reexamining Rather's reportage on that fateful day back in 1963, it's clear there was no way he could have been 100 percent sure John F. Kennedy was dead. As *Time* magazine put it: "His aggressiveness almost got him into trouble. Based on unconfirmed reports from the hospital, Rather told his bosses in New York City that Kennedy had died, leading CBS radio to report the news more than half an hour before the official announcement was made. The bulletin turned out to be correct, much to Rather's relief. . . ."

Tough decision for a reporter. Either announce that the leader of the free world has been assassinated, or wait for the official word. Waiting might be the prudent decision, but it's called "news" for a reason. It's perishable. Quite a dilemma, but, based on heads-up, on-the-fly reporting under a severe deadline, Dan's gut told him he was hearing the truth from people too stressed and confused to concoct lies, so he rolled with the story.

His balls-to-the-wall judgment paid off. He'd go down in history as the reporter who broke the news that JFK, the most idolized president of the twentieth century, had been shot and killed. If he'd gotten it wrong, Dan Rather would have ended up as a footnote in journalism history, a Wrong-Way Corrigan joke and the subject of cautionary "look before you leap" tales told to frighten young reporters.

Instead, he got it right.

In 1964, Rather's lucky break won him the big enchilada—a coveted promotion to the White House beat. But once he hit the big time, his reputation began to fray a bit around the edges. In *The Boys on the Bus,* reporter Timothy Crouse's book about covering presidential campaigns in the Nixon era, Dan's methods came under sharp attack. Wrote Crouse:

> Rather would go with an item even if he didn't have it completely nailed down with verifiable facts. If a rumor sounded solid to him, if he believed in his gut or had gotten it from a man who struck him as honest, he would let it rip. The other White House reporters hated Rather for this. They knew exactly why he got away with it: being handsome as a cowboy, Rather was a star at CBS News, and that gave him the clout he needed. [The White House press corps] could quote all his lapses from fact.

Like the time he reported, erroneously, that J. Edgar Hoover had stepped down as FBI director. Rather, as recent events have shown, waxes even feistier when proven wrong. None of that wimpy, "once bitten, twice shy" stuff for him. Not long after his Hoover gaffe, he again reported that the top G-Man had decamped. Again, he was wrong.

Good reporters are often aggressive, but Rather went way over the top—and nearly got himself fired—when he launched his notoriously arrogant, stupid, and meaningless verbal assault on President Richard M. Nixon during a press conference in 1974. The president had just recognized an

ABC reporter, who barely got his mouth open before Rather butted in and boomed:

"Thank you, Mr. President. Dan Rather of CBS News. Mr. President, with respect . . ."

As Nixon swiveled to react to the out-of-order interruption, the crowd of reporters booed and jeered Rather's brazen behavior. Over the hubbub, Nixon said jokingly, "Are you running for something?"

Snapped Rather, "No, Mr. President, are you?"

The crowd gasped. Rather's crack was beyond rude. It was downright pugnacious, disrespectful to a sitting president— not to mention totally incomprehensible. It was also flat-out dumb for a reporter covering the White House to needlessly antagonize the man who lives there. Ruminating on Rather's question the assembled scribes kept asking one another: What the hell does that even *mean?*

No one has ever answered that question. If Dan himself is cognizant of what was percolating through his lizard brain that fateful day, he's never explained it. But the question CBS executives asked themselves after their Washington correspondent sassed the president of the United States was: "Should we fire the SOB?"

NBC's Tom Brokaw claims CBS considered hiring him to replace Rather, then backed off when word leaked to the press. Another consideration that militated against firing their troublesome correspondent was the approaching retirement of veteran anchorman Walter Cronkite. Texas Dan was the network's lone star. So, the not-quite-saddle-broke maverick survived. And from that moment on, he's been secure in the rock-solid belief that his bosses at what was once known, so quaintly, as the Tiffany Network, would always forgive their diamond-in-the-rough for the lousy judgment his barely suppressed rage often generated.

One jaw-dropping fiasco occurred in 1980. A California doctor charged he'd been wrongly implicated in an insurance fraud scam during a *60 Minutes* report, and dragged CBS and Rather into court. The trial got huge publicity, and CBS bosses groaned as their star was grilled on the witness stand. After the trial, a TV reporter who'd unsuccessfully begged Rather for an interview ambushed him—*60 Minutes*-style—as the anchor walked into the CBS building. Rather shot the guy a loony-toons grin and said, "Sure."

As the reporter got into position for his cameraman, Rather told him: "Get that microphone right up, will you?"

The minute the camera rolled, Dan's bile spewed up like an oil strike from hell as he evil-eyed the reporter and snarled: "F— you! You got it?"

Everybody in America got it! The outrageous "F— you!" video clip—which played like a scene from *The Exorcist*—aired endlessly on nationwide television, mercifully bleeped but explicitly clear. And that's when the snit hit the Dan! Once again, his horrified CBS bosses huddled, but Cronkite was now just a year away from retirement. Under pressure, Rather crafted an apology to the reporter, which led off with a Texas-sized jaw-dropper of a lie. Explained Dan: "I mistook who you were and what you were doing."

Comprende, media fans? Journalist Dan's rather bizarre assertion is that he didn't recognize a guy thrusting a mike in his kisser and asking questions as . . . a journalist?!

Whew! What's the frequency, Kenneth?

Dan went on to allow that mouthing "F— you" into a TV camera was "inexcusable, rude and un-Christian behavior, for which I am remorseful."

It was an MTV moment, as defiant and defining as Jim Morrison of The Doors exposing himself onstage or Jimi Hendrix burning his guitar. Swift on its heels came yet another rock-on revelation that forever ensconced Dan Rather in the pop culture pantheon: He admitted he'd experimented with drugs—hard drugs. Shock and horror reverberated across our great land when, that very same year, the successor to Walter Cronkite admitted, not to *High Times* magazine, but to staid, mainstream *Ladies Home Journal:*

"I had someone at the Houston police station shoot me with heroin so I could do a story about it."

Beyond the impact of his astounding revelation, note Dan's blithe assertion that reporters should seek subjective experience to report competently on illegal acts. It would be akin to me, while writing my book on the O. J. Simpson Trial, persuading a policeman at the Los Angeles jail to break God knows how many laws and supply me with a knife and an expendable guinea-pig prisoner to slice and dice so I could better understand how it feels to commit murder. Once again, Dangerous Dan danced on the edge of reason. Did he really believe getting a cop to jab a spike into his veins somehow made him a better reporter? Or is he truly a freak, a thrill junkie?

"The experience was a special kind of hell," he told his

interviewer. "I came out understanding full well how one could be addicted to 'smack'—and quickly."

One imagines the ladies at *Ladies Home Journal* shuddering, but in a flash, Dan topped even that eye-opening admission. "As a reporter—and I don't want to say that that's the only context—I've tried everything," he confessed. "I can say to you with confidence I know a fair amount about LSD. I've never been a social user of any of these things, but my curiosity has carried me into a lot of interesting areas."

The anchorman, who'd by that time been married for years to wife Jean, was asked about their two young children in an era of widespread drug use. He answered: "I told them . . . if you're hell-bent to try pot, and I suspect you will be, then try it at home around people who care about you."

Say what?

Dan Rather coming on hip about "smack" and "acid"? Encouraging his offspring to toke the smoke at home? The message reverberated loud and clear in Middle America: This was not your father's anchorman! In Portage, Indiana, population 21,000, the city council passed a unanimous resolution against Dan Rather becoming the successor to Cronkite on CBS "because he has acknowledged experimenting with drugs," the *New York Times* reported.

The resolution's author, Leon West, said it came about when he and two fellow council members were at the local police station witnessing the cops hauling in prisoners from a big drug bust. "We got to looking through the newspaper," he recalled, "and here's Dan Rather saying it's OK to use drugs."

Dan copping about drugs to the prissy *Ladies Home Journal* was weird. Stranger yet, he stonewalled when hit with similar questions from swinging *Playboy* magazine a year earlier in 1979.

PLAYBOY: Have you ever smoked marijuana?
RATHER: I prefer not to answer that one.
PLAYBOY: Have you ever snorted cocaine?
RATHER: I prefer not to answer that, too. . . .

If Dan Rather, managing editor of CBS News, heard those exact interview responses from a politician, he'd immediately order a team of reporters to start digging for solid evidence of drug abuse. And he'd probably hit the Houston police station himself to nail down the hottest story of all: Exposing a cop who had apparently stolen heroin from a police evidence locker then broken the law by injecting it into said politician.

Put another way, why shouldn't Rather be grilled by his CBS News bosses and asked: Dan, what makes you think you're above the law? And how can we ever again trust your reporting about the police—you know they could expose your illegal drug use if you ever crossed them. Don't you realize the police may have secretly videotaped you getting shot up with "smack," to use your vernacular?

Never gonna happen, as President Bush 41 would put it. Anchor elites are way, way above the law, even if politicians are not. In the late '90s, I happened to be watching when ABC's Sam Donaldson on *This Week* asked former Senator

Bill Bradley if he'd ever used illegal drugs. Bradley confessed he'd smoked marijuana, then smartly turned the tables on Sam and fired back: "Have you?"

Caught by surprise, Donaldson admitted reluctantly, "I think a couple of times I've tried it. And I inhaled."

Despite the intimations of high times in Anchor Land, here's an insight from the *Playboy* interview that reveals how Dan values high standards above even the best things in life.

> PLAYBOY: What's better than sex?
> RATHER: Nothing. No, let me amend that. Honor is better than sex.

The interview yielded yet another of Dan's trademark, *faux* folksy ramblings.

> PLAYBOY: Do you have any heroes?
> RATHER: Yes [Rather names newsmen Eric Sevareid, Walter Cronkite, etc.], but without being preachy about it, let me tell you who I really like. I love the guy who goes to work every morning, comes home every night, brings his pay check in every week, breaks his ass for his kids and ends up dead at 57. And out of my high school class of roughly 400, at least 200 of them are like that.

Dan's diligent about burnishing his carefully crafted image as a down-home, folksy fella—who just happens to earn $10 million a year. He loves reminding people, in that terse Texas twang, that he's just a worker bee, y'all. Here's a man who inhabits the power position in a Manhattan skyscraper that beams news to the world, a man who literally answers to no one. Yet he'd have us believe he's just a simple laborer, clutching his sombrero and cowering as he anticipates the crack of the overseer's whip. Here's how Dan sums up his working life:

"I get off the truck in the morning and I ask two questions: Who is the boss and what is it that he wants?"

Just a humble toiler like the next man, eh, Dan? The pious homilies that bubble up endlessly from this self-dramatizing *force majeur* of a man have never lulled his CBS News colleagues into making the dire mistake of treating him like one of the boys. Behind his back, they call him "Anchor monster."

In reportage by Eleanor Randolph in the *Washington Post Magazine* back in 1990, a colleague says: "He comes in many layers, like a three-dimensional game of chess." There's Dan the well-scrubbed anchorman, and there's What's-the-Frequency Dan, "the tense, mercurial person who seems to emit strange subliminal vibes that wackos hear . . . and Gentleman Dan, the thoughtful, patriotic Texan . . . whose eyes well with tears over the waving of an American flag."

And there's Dan Machiavelli, the ambitious, savvy corporate infighter who battled up from a Houston slum, knifed every city slicker in sight, then plunked his ass into Walter Cronkite's fabled Chair of Power. And, lest we forget, there's Dan Reporter, who exudes overconfidence, but often adds substance to the stories he delivers. It's when his overconfidence explodes into hot-tempered arrogance that Dan disgraces himself and embarrasses the journalistic enterprise he heads as managing editor. The unforgettable—and for many TV journalists, unforgivable—example of Dan's self-indulgent, puerile posturing was the time he committed the unspeakable broadcasting crime, storming off the set and leaving his network *black* for six minutes!

Six minutes doesn't sound like much, but in broadcast time it's . . . eternity. Once you command the airwaves, the—pardon the pun—immutable law is that you must fill them with sounds and/or pictures. Constantly. Endlessly. No one knows that better than Dan. It's reflected unmistakably in the title of his autobiography *The Camera Never Blinks.*

The infamous desertion of the anchor desk occurred on September 11, 1987. In Miami to cover a visit by the pope, Dan started getting testy when word filtered down that network honchos might extend the time of the semifinal tennis match in the U.S. Open they were airing, thereby eating into his news broadcast. Dan simmered, then warned that he wouldn't tolerate a sports event encroaching on the inviolable start time of his evening news. As the clock ticked and the tennis balls volleyed, he finally uttered the threat rarely heard in broadcasting: "I'll walk off!"

CBS management never blinked, not believing Dan truly meant it. That turned out to be a costly miscalculation. When the match ran over, rage-blinded Rather ran for the exit, threatening to call CBS uber-honcho Howard Stringer to complain. Moments later, as the tennis match finally concluded, network technicians in New York switched to the Miami feed, and got . . . nothing!

Panic ensued! Incredibly, no one had the presence of mind to do what's usually done in such an emergency: slap on a pretaped segment about the pope, or a commercial, or a public service announcement—anything! Unbelievably, CBS viewers were staring at blank screens.

In the aftermath of this unprecedented debacle, world headlines—bad ones—popped up like a dandelions after spring rain, as Dan might put it. Big Daddy Walter Cronkite—once known as the most trusted man in America—socked it to his CBS successor when asked his opinion about the brouhaha. "I can answer that [question] in five words: I would have fired him. . . . There's no excuse for it. The news department doesn't own the network. Compromises have to be made."

Note that Uncle Walter, the one newsman alive who might qualify for the pontifical post of high priest of journalism, gets right to the point. Reporting the news is a job, like any other. It's not a lofty profession, it's a craft. Like brick-laying. Or carpentry. You gather your raw materials, you build your story. Period.

Cronkite rightly intuited that the crux of Rather's petulant dereliction of duty was a pious belief that news is somehow sacrosanct, and he its holy prelate. You should listen to Cronkite, Dan. He knows that news is first and foremost a business. The network moguls who control your sacred CBS News—that hallowed rectory once occupied by Cronkite and the revered Edward R. Murrow—are in the business of making money. Watch what happens if advertising dollars someday sink below the bottom line. You think the camera never blinks, Dan? The day the network can't afford you, your camera will blink . . . *off!*

Another major slam skewering his holiness for Walk-off-gate arrived by overseas delivery from the assiduous *Times* of London. In a shock headline about the dead-air incident, the stately *Times* asked, in impeccable American slang: "Is Dan Rather, bishop of the nation's news business, losing his marbles?"

Well, they called him "bishop," at least. Perhaps he is holy, after all.

USA Today wrote a major piece about the walk-off that included an in-depth look at Dan's history of strange behavior and his slowly sinking ratings. It was headlined: "Rather's Roller Coaster: The Agony and the Anchorman." It dredged up incidents that were making headlines at the time, like Dan's unexplained bombshell contention that recently deceased CIA director William Casey might not be dead after all.

In February 1988, *Time* magazine reported: "In an interview during last summer's Iran-*contra* hearings, [Rather] peppered former CIA Chief William Colby with questions about the rumor—taken seriously by almost no one else—that the late CIA director William Casey was not really dead."

Then there was Dan's nasty, off-the-wall report on the release of former ABC newsman Charles Glass, who'd escaped terrorists holding him hostage in Lebanon. *Time* reported that Rather "sounded a jarring note of skepticism, referring to Glass as 'a young American who says he was a hostage.'" ABC's courtly *Nightline* anchorman Ted Koppel reacted in uncharacteristic fury to Rather's sneaky innuendo that the kidnapping of their reporter might have been a hoax and delivered the stinging retort that the CBS newsman's vicious, unsupported implication was "beneath contempt!"

The headlines trumpeting Dan's desertion of his news post finally faded, as headlines always do. But just six months later, he shocked the nation again during a bristling, aggressive *CBS Evening News* interview with Vice President George Bush, who was making his run for the presidency. Rather detractors have described the interview as "vicious," "brutal," and "rude." And so were the headlines the encounter generated. The *New York Post* painted its entire front page with:

"RATHER BUSHWHACKS VEEP!"

It was more a case of: "Dan Puts Money Where Mouth Is."

Dan makes no bones about espousing in-your-face confrontation with his interviewees—especially Republicans. In a speech he once delivered at a convention of radio and TV directors, Dan sneered at reporters who pussyfoot their way through interviews.

"Do powder puff, not probing interviews," he intoned sarcastically. "Stay away from controversial subjects. Kiss ass, move with the mass, and for heaven and ratings' sake, don't make anybody mad—certainly not anyone you're covering, and especially not the mayor, the governor, the senator, the president, or the vice president, or anybody in a position of power. Make nice, not news."

Dan definitely did not make nice with George Bush. And his interview did not yield any "news"—just more headlines that declared him, once again, rude and abrasive. Rather attacked Bush relentlessly on the Iran-Contra scandal, and, as he admits in his follow-up autobiography, *The Camera Never*

Blinks Twice, the interview was described by one TV critic as "like watching two scorpions in a bottle." The clash between the Anchor and the Veep got progressively nastier. At one point, DR and GB had this barbed exchange:

> DR: I don't want to be argumentative, Mr. Vice President.
> GB: You do, Dan.
> DR: No . . . no sir, I don't.

A moment later, George Herbert Walker Bush slipped in the zinger that really hit where it hurt, as Dan later admitted.

> GB: It's not fair to judge my whole career by a rehash on Iran.
> How would you like it if I judged your whole career on
> those seven minutes you walked off the set? How would
> you like that?"
> DR: Well, Mr. . . . .
> GB: Would you like that?
> DR: Mr. Vice President . . .
> GB: I have respect for you, but I don't have respect for what
> you're doing here tonight.

After concluding the interview by cutting off the vice president rather tersely—he'd plead later that they'd suddenly run out if time—Dan stalked off the set, already sensing the tension. He got a hint of just how intense the firestorm was going to get when he encountered Donna Dees, at that time the public relations person for the *CBS Evening News.* Recalled Rather: "I said to Donna, 'Look, are we in trouble with this, and if so, what can we do?' She burst into tears. Let me be honest, that told me more than what I wanted to know. Then she managed to get out one word: 'Apologize.'"

Rather's reaction?

"I turned steel cold right there. I made sure my eyes locked onto hers. 'Wait a minute,' I said. 'I haven't done anything to apologize for, and I'm not apologizing.'"

Dan recalled that as of the next morning, CBS had logged about six thousand calls—running five to one against him. His CBS bosses put heat on him to apologize, but Rather refused.

"I tried not to bristle," he recalled. "'Won't anybody point out,' I asked, 'that he didn't answer the question?'"

Sound familiar? A goodly slice of the American public and his news colleagues believed, based on their eyewitness judgment, that he'd been ill-tempered and rude. Dan dismissed their opinions, as was his prerogative, and responded with that familiar, plaintive plea he used to excuse Rathergate: Ignore my unprofessional methods, please! With respect, answer the question.

To be fair, he was on firmer ground this time. Reporters often need to be aggressive, and being vice president doesn't earn you untouchable, sacred-cow status. But Dan gets the big bucks for his anchoring skills—the ability to control his emotions and stage-manage a newscast with dignity while millions watch. Media critic Ken Auletta, in his history of the Big Three networks, *Three Blind Mice*, observed: "With Walter Cronkite as the model, viewers had come to expect their anchors to perform as gracious hosts, polite, judicious, cool. Instead, they saw the hot, prosecutorial side of Dan's personality."

Mike Wallace, the *60 Minutes* star famed for his own tough interviewing style, said of his CBS colleague: "The style was wrong. Dan lost his cool."

Badgering an interviewee can come off as bullying. And Dan's always suspect because he revels in his tough-guy image. Worse, badgering can strike the viewing audience as pointless. Who's ever seen a TV reporter scare a politician into an on-camera confession of murder, adultery, even spitting on the sidewalk, for that matter? Dan and his CBS producers knew full well that Vice President Bush was never going to answer the all-encompassing Iran-Contra question: What did you know and when did you know it?

The reporter-turned-prosecutor shtick can also backfire, as it did when Bush 41—ever sensitive about his "wimp" image—unexpectedly lashed back and accused Dan of being argumentative. Momentarily shaken, Rather blurted, "You've made us hypocrites in the face of the world."

Whoopsie, Dano! Was that a question? Sounds more like a rather-biased opinion. You've been quoted as saying, "The camera never lies." Well, that's precisely the kind of remark that seems to expose you as a raving left-winger, in the opinion of many. Your stated mission in interviewing Vice President Bush on CBS was to reveal the news—not to stand on your soapbox and proclaim your personal view of world opinion. Stick to the news, pal, or get yourself a talk show. That gives you the leeway to do commentary. I've done it and, trust me, it's lots of fun. On a talk show, you get to bait people, infuriate them, make them scream—then you scream back and pontificate about any damn thing you want! Well, now that I think of it, that's not much different from what you're doing as an anchorman, is it? But spraying opinions like a flame-thrower is not doing legitimate news. It is not conducting oneself as a responsible anchor.

In the firestorm that followed the Bush interview, *Los Angeles Times* TV critic Howard Rosenberg likened Rather's ruthless attack to Captain Queeg in *The Caine Mutiny*. Rosenberg told *Time* magazine: "There was no excuse for him assuming the roles of the judge and jury in a newscast. . . . Who appointed him America's shrieking ayatollah of truth?"

Newsweek headlined its piece with a quote from the embattled anchor: "I Was Trained to Ask Questions." Their subhead: "Combative and high-strung, Dan Rather remains more reporter than anchorman."

In the minds of some, the confrontation apparently helped George Bush win the presidency in 1988 because he finally shook the "wimp" image that had plagued him for his entire political career. Why, he'd stood up to Dan Rather, by God! Reports had Bush swaggering all over the locker room after their TV brawl.

"The bastard didn't lay a glove on me," he crowed to campaign aides. Then he told CBS staffers, "Tell your gawddamned network that if they want to talk to me to raise their hands at a press conference. No more 'Mr. Inside' stuff after that!" He naughtily added—in a quote unheard by viewers, but duly reported by several publications—"He makes [TV newswoman] Leslie Stahl look like a pussy!"

Later, Bush apologized for taking God's name—but not Leslie Stahl's—in vain. And he was as good as his word: he never forgave Rather, never granted him another interview.

The grudge was handed down to son Dubya—Bush 43—who's never deigned to speak to Rather since assuming the presidency.

Once again, Dan Rather had made headlines for being controversial. And once again, he handled the fallout badly. His image suffered; not so much due to the almost universal judgment that he'd, at the least, tippy-toed the fine line between tough and fair but to his reaction to the very suggestion that he'd stepped over it. That creepy, hair-trigger rage always lurking just beneath Dan's thin skin was revealed in the aforementioned overkill response to his public relations person's suggestion that he apologize: "I turned cold steel right there . . .," etc.

Rather took a savage pounding from news colleagues after the Bush interview. Even the pugnacious Sam Donaldson—ABC's foam-at-the-mouth attack dog—snarled, "Rather went too far." In a mind-boggling, pot-calling-the-kettle-black moment, Sam actually accused Dan of "arrogance"!

"Rather went too far . . . I don't think we [as journalists] can get to a situation where we make—on our own authority—accusations."

The question that needed answering kept coming up: Had Rather really snapped? Suddenly, he seemed like an eerie echo of anchorman Howard Beale in the movie *Network*. His inner man was screaming, *I'm mad as hell and I'm not going to take it anymore!*

The unkindest cut of all came in 1989, when the usually docile *TV Guide* published an eyeopener headlined, "Rather Strange: Behind Dan's Odd Behavior." The anchorman had turned down a request to be interviewed for the story, so the writer turned to mental-health experts for answers about his years of odd behavior. One analysis truly infuriated Rather (he called it "bullfeathers!"). Famed Los Angeles psychiatrist David Viscott offered comment on repeated incidents of total strangers attacking the anchorman; like the guy who beat him mercilessly while asking, "What's the frequency, Kenneth?" And then there was the bizarre incident—related in Peter J. Boyer's book *Who Killed CBS?*—that occurred at Kennedy Airport in New York.

"Rather was walking through a crowded area . . . there was some jostling, and a man suddenly approached him and just knocked him down flat. He's the kind of person things seem to happen to!"

Then there was another strange encounter, reported by the *New York Times:* "A cabby picked up Dan Rather . . . at Chicago's O'Hare Airport yesterday, and things began to happen. According to a spokesman for the Chicago police, the cab driver refused to go where he was told and instead 'drove wildly through the streets' with Mr. Rather shouting and gesturing for help."

In the *TV Guide* story, Dr. Viscott explained that in psychiatry there is a general rule that "What you get back is a reflection of what you give . . . there must be something about what he does that causes anger in other people."

Rather was quoted as retorting, "They have never met me and they give their analyses of me."

Yet it's true *The Camera Never Blinks* is peppered with incidents of people threatening him, punching him—even pulling guns on him. One woman who confronted him on an airplane hissed, "Somewhere, you are going to get yours. If I have to arrange it, I will."

Behavioral experts quoted in *TV Guide* espoused various theories about what makes Dan tick . . . tick . . . tick . . . like a time bomb. One likened him to a high-spirited racehorse that blows off steam by occasionally taking a healthy kick at the barn door. Another labeled him the victim of "failed ghost-buster syndrome," because he'd never been able to exorcise the formidable specter of Walter Cronkite, which still loomed large over the CBS anchor chair. It's a theory others have held, but which Rather denies.

"I'm not Cronkite," he was quoted as saying in *Parade* magazine. "My job is to be a good Dan Rather. Cronkite was one of a kind—the best there ever has been at what he did. There may not be anybody who is that good at it again."

There's no doubt Rather revered—and feared—Cronkite (who mysteriously was never asked to guest on CBS News, not even for *auld lang syne*). When he replaced him in 1981, Dan immediately displayed his penchant for bizarre behavior. In *Who Killed CBS?* Boyer reported that rookie Rather refused to seat himself in the retired anchor's chair during his very first newscast. Incredibly, he insisted on crouching behind Cronkite's desk instead.

For anyone who didn't live through the Cronkite era, who never bore witness to how the dignified anchorman solemnly guided America through the JFK assassination in those first hours of numb disbelief, it's difficult to comprehend what the CBS icon signified to the nation. No one remotely like him exists today. More than a newsman, both the common man and the world's leaders respected him as an elder statesman. It was Cronkite, remember, who single-handedly achieved the impossible in the Middle East, bringing blood enemies Anwar Sadat of Egypt and Menachem Begin of Israel together for face-to-face talks. His influence was overwhelming. When he filed a critical report on America's conduct of the Vietnam War, President Lyndon Johnson remarked, "If I've lost Cronkite, I've lost middle America!"

Just months after succeeding Cronkite in 1981, Rather lost Middle America—or a goodly chunk of it. CBS News ratings began to slide. The nation had taken its first look at the new anchorman, and apparently wasn't warming up to what it saw.

In October of that year, *Parade* magazine—a publication aimed at Main Street USA—took the nation's pulse and reported: "Rumors persist that Rather will not last long as anchor at CBS, that he is the wrong man for the job. His critics say that the intensity and drive that got him where he is will also be his undoing—that his intense ambition to succeed comes across in a way that makes viewers nervous."

Rather didn't totally disagree with the analysis, countering that he's simply "determined, interested and enthusiastic. . . . I don't feel intense. I like this job. I want to do well at it. And I think my wanting to do well comes across. And some people may interpret that as a certain intensity. . . . If that's what people are picking up, that's accurate. I know news. I know stories. I don't yet know everything about anchoring I want to know. I'm certainly not as good at it as I want to be."

Then, reaching into that apparently bottomless bag of down-home homilies, Dan intoned: "I learned a long time ago that I'm not a racehorse. I'm a workhorse. And I'll get your field plowed for you—maybe not as fast as some others—but I'll get there."

Brave talk. But did slow and steady win the race? You be the judge! Nine years later, *Newsday* reported, in an in-depth piece about the CBS star, that he'd finally scored a huge triumph by nailing down a ninety-minute interview with infamous dictator Saddam Hussein. As *Newsday* put it, "For once, people were taking notice of Rather for all the *right* reasons. He wouldn't be in the next day's headlines because some weirdo had chased him down the street, demanding, 'Kenneth, what's the frequency?' Or because he had stormed off the set, as he had done in Miami . . . or because he had a shouting match with a presidential candidate—on *live* TV."

So far . . . Rather good.

Yet in the same piece, *Newsday* noted: "To many viewers, this anchorman has often looked like he is about to explode right into their living rooms. The tight-lipped smile, the stiff bearing, the hard, forced friendliness always have seemed to many a form of blatant phoniness—but to people who know him, Rather is simply out of his element as anchor. He is not comfortable. . . . He has taken voice lessons, worked on the smile, and once even wore sweaters to soften his image."

Style's one thing, substance another. Dan Rather's never been accused of being a fashion plate, despite the tailored suits that comprise any working anchor's work uniform *du jour*. Neither was Walter Cronkite, but the wily TV icon proved over a brilliant career that substance always earns respect. That lesson was sometimes lost on Dan.

In 1988, Rather came under heavy attack from military experts who opened fire after the airing of his one-hour special "CBS Reports: The Wall Within." It was an ambitious documentary that investigated the bizarre lifestyle of Vietnam veterans living wild in the forests of Washington State. By Rather's account, these were brave men—heroes, even— whose spirit and sanity had been broken by their horrific experiences in the war's dark jungles. "The Wall Within" didn't merely sound dramatic. The show delivered, big-time! Dan conducted searing interviews with ex-GIs, who told of committing unspeakable atrocities while serving under the American flag. CBS touted the news special as "the rebirth of the documentary."

One of these veterans interviewed by Dan—Terry Bradley, described as "a fighting sergeant"—related a stomach-turning tale of how he'd skinned fifty still-living Vietnamese men, women, and children in just one hour and then stacked their bodies like so much cordwood. Millions of viewers were riveted as Bradley said: "Could you do this for one hour of your life? You stack up every way a body could be mangled, up into a body, an arm, a tit, an eyeball . . . imagine us over there for a year and doing it intensely . . . that is sick."

Responded Dan sympathetically: "You've got to be angry about it."

Good newsmen are not cynics, but should always be skeptics. It's hard to believe that Dan, who endlessly reminds us he's a rock-ribbed Texas country boy, didn't reply, "Hoss, that dog won't hunt!" Even if Dan had never hunted or dressed game back in Texas, alarm bells should have started clanging when Bradley started expounding on that whopping claim of slaughtering and skinning approximately one human being per minute. As one of the last kids in America who ran trap lines and sold furs to Sears Roebuck, I promise you that trying to skin even fifty small animals in an hour would be a mind-boggling, if not impossible, task. And common sense should've tipped Dan that skinning a live human being writhing in pain is . . . well, it's a damn lie that wouldn't fool most city boys, much less a sensible old Texan.

Yet Dan never challenged Bradley, never used his journalistic common sense. Does that mean Dan is bereft of common sense? No. What it means—to any competent journalist/editor who makes a living feeding raw facts through truth's wringer—is that Dan was probably suffering from an all-too-common affliction: he'd fallen head-over-heels in love with a sensational story, and he didn't have the heart to challenge it, lest it fall apart. There's an old newsroom jibe that goes:

Never lets facts stand in the way of a good story.

It's a joke that's actually a sarcasm-cloaked warning—a mantra that's supposed to spring from our journalistic subconscious and shake us awake whenever, with thumping hearts, we clutch too hotly at some dreamy little scoop. Two variations of the same theme are often repeated in newsrooms:

Never fall in love with a story. There's always another one coming right down the road behind it.

And:

Never lose sleep over an item.

Dan's heard all these warnings. Every newsman has. Yet he ignored them. Why? It's awfully hard for any news professional to believe that he and his CBS News team never thought about checking military records. Laziness? Maybe. Or was it that falling-in-love syndrome? The fear of discovering that these sensational tales were too "good" to be true? Had Dan checked military records—as did Vietnam veteran and expert B. G. Burkett, author of the acclaimed book, *Stolen Valor*—he'd have uncovered some eyeopening facts. For instance, "fighting sergeant" Terry Bradley was an outrageous liar who'd never seen combat. In fact, Bradley spent one year in a military jail for going AWOL. His actual job: ammo handler in the 25th Infantry Division.

Author Burkett's embarrassing probe of Dan's platoon of Vietnam phonies—who claimed that the horrors of combat had driven them to drink, drugs and the mental torture of suicidal thoughts—exposed a catalogue of lies. Among them:

- The Navy Seal "assassin," who claimed he'd murdered Vietnamese civilians to make it look like Viet Cong were committing atrocities, proved to be an equipment repairman. Turns out he'd never been near a combat zone and actually served time in the brig for repeated AWOL.
- The "combat vet" who'd sobbed as he recalled cradling a

dying buddy blown in half by a grenade was unmasked as a total phony. Records proved he'd actually served as a military policeman—and never got anywhere near a battlefield.

• The sailor who described being sprayed by the blood of a shipmate chopped up by a spinning propeller aboard the aircraft carrier Ticonderoga turned out to be a total con. The truth: there was a man killed by a propeller on the Ticonderoga—but the sailor who told Dan the tale hadn't witnessed it. And the Ticonderoga was actually on a training mission off the coast of California, not "a secret mission off Vietnam."

And on . . . and on. . . .

Memory fades fast. Even people in the news business now have dim recollection of Rather's documentary debacle and his repeated stonewalling when confronted by Burkett with facts based on his search of military records. And why did Dan stonewall? Because he didn't have the courage to admit he'd committed an unpardonable journalistic sin. A routine search of military records should have been made by Rather's highly paid news team; he, as managing editor, should have demanded it.

Sounds just like Dan's present-day problem, doesn't it? Military records . . . basic facts not checked . . . bogus sources . . . stonewalling in the face of contrary evidence . . . denial, denial, denial!

Writing in the *National Review,* Anne Morse dubbed this shabby episode, "The First Rathergate." Morse notes that after

Burkett shared his findings with CBS, so did Thomas Turnage, then administrator of the Veterans Administration, who was appalled by Rather's use of bogus statistics on the rates of suicide, homelessness and mental illness among Vietnam veterans—statistics that can also easily be checked. Rather initially refused to comment. . . . For his part, CBS President Howard Stringer defended the network with irrelevancies. "Your criticisms were not shared by a vast majority of our viewers," Stringer sniffed, adding that "CBS News and its affiliates received acclaim from most quarters. . . . There are no apologies to make."

Say what?

With respect, Mr. Stringer, answer the question! Was your "acclaimed" documentary a pack of lies or *not?*

Enquiring minds want to know.

Harking back to the journalistic maxim that warns against falling in love with a story, let me add this caution: You should fall out of love immediately if solid evidence surfaces to disprove it. To quote Ms. Morse: "As angry Vietnam veterans began calling CBS to complain about the factual inaccuracies of 'The Wall Within,' Perry Wolff, the executive producer who wrote the documentary, claimed that 'No one has attacked us on the facts.' Despite the growing evidence that he'd been had, Rather also continued to defend the documentary."

Just as he defended the indefensible Rathergate!

Chapter 3

Is Dan Rather a journalist—or does he just play one on TV?
"Hear ye, hear ye! Draw near for the Trial of Dan Rather!"

Actually, that's just a TV-style tease to keep you hooked.
We're not quite ready to bang the opening gavel. To extend
the trial metaphor, our case is still "in discovery." This is the
grand jury phase, in which we'll continue our exhaustive,
hopefully not exhausting, examination of Dan Rather's journalistic track record. Our aim: to pinpoint the factors that
shaped the star anchor's approach to newsgathering.

First, let's compare the medium of television journalism to
print. Television news is all about "the look." It runs on a star
system of pretty people and rock-solid authority figures
beaming at you with a package of moving pictures—which
had better be "moving" in every sense of the word. Famed
60 Minutes creator Don Hewitt once explained to a Columbia
University journalism class that TV can't come alive without
the visual elements and the right personality: "A writer in a
magazine can use his writing talents to make the [story] interesting. Not in television. In television, dull is dull is dull."

That's an acknowledged, Emmy-winning legend speaking,
expertly summing up the essence of television. Looking for a
career in TV news? If you're cute enough, or glib enough, go

for an on-camera career. If not, you can try producing—but you'd better be endlessly brilliant at dreaming up sexy visuals that'll jazz the screen.

In fact, TV—the small screen—has much in common with the so-called silver screen. A television superstar like Dan Rather needs exactly what movie superstar Tom Cruise needs: great stories illustrated by dramatic moving pictures. Dialogue is important, for sure, but the screen won't glow without riveting visuals swirling around a sexy, larger-than-life star. Dan and Tom didn't hit the big time based on story-telling talent alone. These guys get the big bucks because they make ladies swoon. Print journalists, rarely photogenic, rarely get rich. Our careers don't rise or fall on the swoon factor. If our words crack thunder, we prosper—albeit invisibly.

The pace of TV journalism is insane. I have had some experience in producing for television and often caution my print colleagues—who imagine it's a terribly glamorous world—to be careful what they wish for. To repeat Hewitt's excellent analysis, print journalists can massage a so-so story to life just by sheer writing talent. In TV, "dull is dull is dull." That's why small-screen journalism lives or dies on the strength of its moving pictures. Dramatic footage is crucial, and producers are driven to deliver it. Sometimes, however, they crack under the strain, which is apparently what happened in 1980, when Hewitt disguised Rather in flowing robes and a funny hat, then slipped him into Afghanistan to star in a derring-do desert drama as dashing, daring "Gunga Dan!"

In the book *Tick . . . Tick . . . Tick . . .: The Long Life and Turbulent Times of 60 Minutes,* author David Blum says it was

Rather himself who conceived the idea of infiltrating Afghanistan to report on a faraway war that average Americans weren't much concerned about. When he first proposed the amateur-theatrical premise as a serious *60 Minutes* piece, producer Hewitt initially told him, "Forget it!"

Good thinking.

Unfortunately, Hewitt didn't stick to his instincts. In the news business, even old hands who should know better let themselves get sweet-talked into doing what are known as "You are there!" stories—the kind of self-indulgent crap a wise old editor of mine called "gawddamn travelogues." These are so-called "color" pieces sold on the premise that they'll put the reader or viewer right in the action—but usually have little or no real news value. So you end up with "our fearless reporter" tramping through exotic locales, droning a narcissistic narrative about the hardships he's suffering, the dangers he's braving . . . blah, blah, blah. It sounds something like this: "There I was, paddling through the darkest reaches of the Amazon jungle in a tiny dugout canoe, ducking poisonous snakes dangling from low-hanging branches, knowing one false move could tip me into murky waters teeming with flesh-eating piranha!"

Despite Hewitt's initial resistance, Rather talked the veteran producer into sending him on the story—even though the costs would amount to double the usual budget for a *60 Minutes* piece.

According to Blum: "In typical Rather fashion, 'Inside Afghanistan' quickly became more about Rather than about the horrors he was reporting, whether by accident or design." In other words, what was meant to be a tale of high adventure transmogrified into vintage travelogue. It was marvelous entertainment for snide newsmen everywhere, who chortled at the exploits of swashbuckling "Gunga Dan."

The year was 1980. The Soviet Union, in one of its last hurrahs, had become bogged down in a dirty little war they'd launched to maintain a puppet regime in remote Afghanistan. The average American didn't know much, or care much, about a conflict being fought in the trackless deserts and remote mountain passes of a wild, virtually lawless country. But Don Hewitt, caught up finally in the mad glamour of it all, went to great lengths and smuggled Dan through the Khyber Pass, or wherever, to report on—what?

Oh, sure, it was a war, but it was guerilla warfare—the kind that's largely invisible and doesn't yield dramatic moving pictures. So other than the old, reliable premise that "war is hell," the story really had no angle, at least none that justified dispatching the crown prince of network news. If Hewitt had wanted real news about the war, he could have sent in any competent correspondent. But that, of course, would have been pointless because America had no emotional investment in the Afghanistan battle. No troops of ours were on the ground, or in the air. Our only involvement was in sending supplies to rebel tribesmen, thereby helping to annoy, confound and—who knew?—maybe even defeat our Cold War enemies, the Soviets.

After *60 Minutes* aired the Afghanistan piece, *Washington Post* TV critic Tom Shales filed a devastating report on the exploits of "Gunga Dan" and his dashing disguise. It began:

"Your assignment, Dan, should you agree to accept it, is to

penetrate the Afghanistan border, gain the confidence of resistance fighters there, let your beard grow a few days, wear a funny hat, and file a story for *60 Minutes*."

How did Shales assess the story's news value? "We knew something about the war against the invading Soviet troops before *60 Minutes*, but, and this is important, did we know how the war was affecting Dan Rather?"

Describing Rather's "disguise," the *Washington Post* critic marveled:

Rather wore peasant togs that made him look like an extra out of *Dr. Zhivago*. Vanessa Redgrave wearing the same outfit would have been welcomed at any chic party in Europe. Somehow one got the feeling that this was not so much Dan Rather, as Stuart Whitman playing Dan Rather. Or Dan Rather playing Stuart Whitman playing Dan Rather. There is certainly nothing unjournalistic about donning a disguise— although a $50 haircut still looks like a $50 haircut even when mussed up a little.

Viewing the footage—you can find it on the Internet—is a howl. The CBS star approaches grizzled desert tribesmen and says, "Hello . . . my name is *Rather*."

In the grand and glorious tradition of the "gawddamn travelogue," Gunga Dan blathers endlessly into the camera about how hard he's working, how tough he's having it. Describing the "ordeal" in *The Camera Never Blinks Twice*, Rather writes: "We were slipping and sliding, falling and crawling . . . when, wham, I slipped at top speed and hit my groin hard. . . . I doubled over in pain and thought I might faint. Mirwaz half picked me up, half made me get up. 'Must keep running,' he said with heavy breath. 'Must keep running!'"

He breathlessly told viewers how he'd made a "two-day walk" and made a climb that was "straight up, ten thousand feet." He kept repeating that the Afghans were doomed unless help came soon, as the British cavalry did in the movie classic *Gunga Din*.

Shales concluded his report on Gunga Dan with this snarky summation: "Was it all a story about the war in Afghanistan, or a story about the courage and gallantry of someone out of 'Foreign Correspondent'—Danny Do-Right, ace reporter? . . . The war goes on . . . but at least, thank God, Dan Rather is safe!"

Piranha teeth cannot strip a journalist's flesh faster than a journalist's typewriter. Then, as now, Dan Rather stoically absorbed the lumps delivered by lower-paid, ink-stained print newsies, who admittedly love the blood sport of needling overpaid TV talking heads. And Rather's probable take on us, if he thinks about it at all, is probably: "What the hell do they know? Is Mike Walker making $10 million a year?" Good point, hoss.

Yet there are those who rise quickly to defend Dan, like Marvin Kalb, a former NBC correspondent, who said in *USA Today:* "The very fact that he works so hard, so very intensely, is a credit to his integrity."

Maybe. It could also be proof that, as he's often accused, Dan Rather is an overly aggressive control freak. And working hard, while commendable, is not the same thing as working smart.

Blum, who interviewed many CBS sources in his book, says

Dan suffers from the syndrome identified by CBS wise guys as ADATT—All Dan, All The Time. The anchor insists on hogging the camera, and does not play well with others.

"It's gotten to the point where he would be very happy if he were the only person doing every story," said Blum. "He suffers from an excessive desire to be on TV, and he's infatuated with the red light. . . . One person can't do it all, and there's a price to pay."

The Afghanistan story got even weirder, as things often do with Dan. After his return to the States, the *New York Times* reported astounding news: Gunga Dan had been accused of murder!

Said the *Times:* "The Soviet press agency *Tass* reported today that an Afghan newspaper had accused a CBS News correspondent, Dan Rather, of participating in the murder of three villagers while he was in Afghanistan in March."

Rather, not surprisingly, denied the murder charge. He waxed—and one can hardly blame him, quite indignant about the shocking accusation. He felt, as George W. Bush sometimes does, that he'd been the victim of irresponsible journalism.

Apparently, *Tass* had picked the story up from an Afghan newspaper, which described an execution that allegedly occurred while Dan and his CBS crew were filming. The report read: "The workers were taken to the village square and here one of the U.S. newsmen took charge, ordering the bandits first to stone the captives and then to cut off their heads. The whole of the bloody sequence was . . . filmed by the Americans."

Tass quoted the Afghan paper: "It becomes absolutely clear that Rather, the CBS-TV commentator, participated in the bloody murder of three Afghan workers." Rather told the *Times* he'd seen no such incident. He slammed the *Tass* report as "fantasy from first letter to last, sheer unadulterated nonsense." The charge was ludicrous, to be sure. But once again, out of nowhere and for no apparent reason, a vicious attack had been visited on Dan Rather, TV's poster boy for weird karma.

In *The Camera Never Blinks Twice*, Rather boasts that after his return, radio reports out of Pakistan and Moscow mentioned rewards "of many thousand of dollars" for his death or capture.

"I was honored," he said proudly.

Dan was assuming—correctly, I'm sure—that the price on his head was testament to the pain he'd inflicted on the bad guys with his brave, truthful reporting. Or was it simply the usual dead-or-alive reward for a wanted murderer? (I'm kidding, of course.)

Speaking of avoiding stories that, like Dan's Afghanistan foray, are actually a "gawddamn travelogue" in disguise, here's a footnote from my own experience that still astounds me and *National Enquirer* colleagues who recall the tale. It occurred in 1977, just after the phenomenal success of the TV miniseries *Roots*, which still stands as the highest-rated drama in television history. It ran eight nights and was viewed by an astounding 130 million Americans.

The creation of African-American author Alex Haley, *Roots* was supposedly based on a true story—passed down in Haley's family since the 1700s—about their ancestor Kunta Kinte, captured near a jungle village by slave traders and shipped to America as a young man.

The miniseries sparked a nationwide fascination with genealogy that built to a near frenzy. Suddenly, millions of Americans were searching fervidly for their own roots, and eating up stories about the phenomenon in newspapers, magazines, and on TV. Gene Pope, the legendary founder of the *National Enquirer,* pushed our staff hard for sensational story ideas that would feed the craze. One of us—I don't remember who—brainstormed a classic *Enquirer* stunt: We'd launch an expedition to find Kunta Kinte's village, deep in the African jungle, and check the truth of Haley's tale. It was a huge undertaking, costing well over two hundred thousand dollars. Our team of reporters flew to Africa, hired native bearers, and set off through thick, remote jungle hauling—are you ready, tabloid fans?—heavy film projection equipment and a generator powerful enough to power it so we could screen *Roots* in the jungle. There we were, hacking our way through the impenetrable African jungle, hearing the roars of lions and leopards all around us. . . .

Wow! Eat your heart out, Gunga Dan!

The *Enquirer* expedition took weeks, but our team finally hacked through thick jungle and found the village with the help of guides. Incredibly, the natives excitedly told our interpreters that that, yes, Kunta Kinte had actually existed. The story of his abduction had been handed down over the centuries!

So on that first night in the village, after the sun went down, an expedition of *Enquirer* reporters (who apparently were not wearing actual native garb, but costumes vaguely reminiscent of Stewart Granger in *King Solomon's Mines)* actually projected the miniseries *Roots,* which we'd had con-

verted to film, on a screen erected outdoors in a large clear-
ing. The natives went *nuts.*

They'd never seen motion pictures before and reacted with
awe as interpreters made them understand that these "magic
pictures" were a dramatization of Kunta Kinte's real-life
ordeal as a slave in the American South. As one reporter
quipped later: "Shame we never thought of bringing *Gone
With the Wind* as a follow-up."

It was what we called at the *Enquirer* a "gee whiz!" story. The
whole newsroom was electrified as news of our successful
expedition finally filtered back from the Dark Continent. I was
the editor in charge of evaluating reams of copy our reporters
were filing via runners dispatched from the village to the near-
est telegraph point. My job was to write a brief evaluation for
Mr. Pope, who was not just the founder/owner, but also the
flint-eyed gatekeeper who literally edited every word that went
into his paper. I had to recommend how the story should be
played—how many parts, what angles to take, photos, etc.

I recommended a three-parter: (1) the expedition's trek
through the jungle, (2) the amazing movie night in the jungle, and (3) first-person reactions from the emotional villagers, with their messages to homeboy Haley, Kunta Kinte's
direct descendant. Plus photos of Kunta Kinte's—and
Haley's—relatives, and the village that looked much the same
as when slave traders snatched the young man, etc.

I sent my evaluation to Pope's office, copying our editor-
in-chief Iain Calder, who actually phoned to congratulate me
on my evaluation. "What an incredible story," he enthused.

Thirty minutes later, my phone rang again.

"Yes, Mr. Pope?"

The boss barked a couple of terse questions at me. After I answered them, he hung up. About ten minutes later, Pope's assistant dropped the story file on my desk. Slashed across my evaluation was a huge "NG" written in his trademark red marker pen, what we called, "The Mark of the Beast."

He'd killed the whole damn story.

Word raced through the newsroom. Within hours, our jungle telegraph had reached Africa, where our triumphant team—after a long trek back to civilization—was waiting to board a plane for America. My phone rang. It was the chief reporter assigned to the expedition. His voice came from across the pond and down the line in a tinny howl of frustration.

"Mike, what the hell happened? How can Mr. Pope kill this great story? We went through hell to get this!"

I had only heard the "why" myself just moments before. Editor-in-chief Calder, looking slightly shell-shocked, had stopped by my desk to tell me. "Gene says it's nothing but a gawddamn travelogue. He says it's too bad our reporters didn't discover from the natives that Kunta Kinte had never existed. *That* would have been a real story, dammit!"

I still haven't recovered from the shock.

We'd laid out two-hundred-thousand-plus in 1977 dollars, and we weren't going to publish? On any paper for which I've ever worked, they'd have run that story just to get mileage out of money spent. But to the late, great Gene Pope, the most ruthless editor I've ever encountered, it was either a story or it wasn't. To him, the two hundred thousand was chump change. It was either an *Enquirer* story, in his judgment, or it was not. Right or wrong, Pope had drilled home his message to us all: "No gawddamn *travelogues!*"

To this day, I think we should have run a story, with photos of Kunta Kinte's village. A three-parter, I now admit, was probably overkill. But the point is, boring readers with windy tales of your own derring-do is a trap to avoid. Pope drove his point home—painfully: Readers expect newsmen to work hard. That's what they pay us for. So never let them see you sweat—and don't wear funny Gunga Dan hats or great-white-hunter costumes.

I still think I was right about running that *Roots* piece, but I learned a lesson that journalists today have forgotten, for the most part, and it will play heavily as we proceed in the Trial of Dan Rather. Here it is, and don't forget it:

Always think of the reader!

Sounds almost childish, doesn't it? It's not. It's the whole point of what we do as journalists. If we're not thinking of the reader, or viewer, what's the point? If not the reader, for whom are we writing? For our bosses? To impress our colleagues in the news world, hoping to attract the offer of a higher-paying job? Not that there's anything wrong with any of that, mind you, as long as you steadfastly adhere to the singular motto that made the *Enquirer* the much-imitated juggernaut it became—an exhortation that was once, to the staff's barely concealed amusement, put on display in our newsroom on a lighted sign that flickered: "Always think of the reader."

Don't sneer, Media Elite. Ignoring this simple rule is precisely how you end up with devastating journalistic screw-ups like Rathergate. Consider the frank admission that *60 Minutes* executive producer Josh Howard made to the *Washington Post*, speaking of Dan Rather's "scoop" based on documents denigrating President Bush's National Guard service:

"We completely abandoned the process of authenticating the documents," confessed Howard.

Eureka! We just hit the mother lode right there, media mavens. CBS "abandoned the process of authenticating." Sadly, Josh Howard does not sate our febrile curiosity with further explanation of *why* his highly paid news team abdicated their responsibilities as journalists. But here's why the "why" is irrelevant: Whether it was incompetence, sloppiness, or fear of thwarting what the staff perceived as a Rather-biased Dubya vendetta, CBS News absolutely was not thinking of its viewers.

Getting it right for the folks who tune in should have been the highest priority. If reporters were asleep at the switch—day-dreaming about getting rich, drunk or laid—Josh Howard should have shaped them up fast. Or fired them even faster. If Howard was guilty of holding back on research because he sensed Dan had fallen in love with the story, he's the hack who should be whacked. All of the above boils down to one of those simple rules to live by that sound simple-minded but can literally change your life: Stop thinking about your boss, your paycheck, or what time you can duck out for the Knicks game. In our game, it's a given you'll probably get a story wrong someday. When it happens, it's soul churning. So, always think of the reader. Do the research, put the facts to the fire of truth. People count on you to deliver news they can trust. If you finally get one wrong, well . . . nobody's perfect, as Joe E. Lewis would say. Getting over a screw-up is tough. Knowing you did your best helps.

But now, as they say in TV, back to our exciting story.

After Dan Rather returned from Afghanistan, he grimly endured the Gunga Dan ribbing from the press. It's quite telling that he never once mentions any of the often sidesplitting criticisms he endured in *The Camera Never Blinks Twice.* If the Court please, I hereby submit that Mr. Rather evidences a singular lack of humor as regards his own august accomplishments as a derring-do purveyor of the serious news.

In 1981, Rather finally won the prize he'd coveted for more than a decade—the anchor chair vacated by the retiring Walter Cronkite. It was a triumphant moment, and he savored it, but it wasn't long before happiness curdled into nagging fear. Ratings for *The CBS Evening News with Dan Rather* took a nosedive. Worse, a cold-eyed businessman named Laurence Tisch suddenly bought CBS and began, as cold-eyed businessmen do, "tweaking" the bottom line.

In 1984, Tisch presided over a massive bloodletting that went on and on, all the way through 1987, laying off thousands of CBS News employees, including more than two dozen star correspondents like Morton Dean, Ike Pappas, Fred Graham, and David Andelman. From a news juggernaut that had maintained bureaus in most major countries, CBS suddenly couldn't afford to station even one correspondent on the continent of Africa. Tisch then sold off CBS Music, the world's biggest record label, plus its book and magazine publishing divisions.

All this made Tisch a very rich boy. But as the *Wall Street Journal* pointed out: "CBS has been stripped in one year of much of what it built in 60, largely at Mr. Tisch's initiative."

Many compared the CBS downsizing to events in the movie *Broadcast News*—a savage satire on the way network TV journalists do business. In the opinion of many, Dan Rather was the real-life model for the character played by Jack Nicholson, a pompous anchorman whose bloated paycheck was considered sacred as the "little people" were ruthlessly chopped.

Legendary *Chicago Tribune* columnist Mike Royko penned a savage anti-Rather piece after he read, as he explained it to his huge audience of readers:

> . . . an op-ed column in the *New York Times* written by Dan Rather, the famous anchor creature. In it, he bemoaned the dismissals of his co-workers, invoked the sainted memory of Edward R. Murrow and wondered whether the bottom line had now become more important to CBS than being a shining beacon of a sacred public trust. And I was about to dash off an angry note to the hard-eyed corporate executives at CBS, when a memory drifted back to me.

Reporter Royko then recalled that while covering the Republican Convention in Detroit and walking the few blocks from his hotel to the convention center each morning, he'd noticed a parade of limousines arriving to transport all the pampered TV anchormen. Royko told his readers:

> Riding those few blocks were guys who were—blow-dried

hair and hype aside—nothing more than reporters. It didn't surprise me . . . anchormen and other TV news stars didn't walk or ride in a cab. It was sort of a statement about how important they were. . . . But nowhere in Rather's *New York Times* article were such indulgences mentioned. Nor did he say anything about his $2 million salary.

Royko—who'd actually underestimated Dan's annual take, in those days, of $3.5 million, or $13,409 per day—reminded the fat-cat anchorman that his hard-eyed bosses might not be forced to chop so many heads were there fewer limo rides, rented mansions, and other high-ticket expense account items spent by the likes of him. Royko pointed out that the going rate for a top-notch reporter (in those days) was about sixty thousand dollars—so about thirty news hustlers could be hired for the price of, say, Dan's salary.

Concluded Royko: "As Rather said in his article: 'Journalism . . . is a light on the horizon. A beacon that helps the citizens of a democracy find their way.' Sure it is, Dan. But most citizens manage to find their way five or six blocks without the help of a limo driver."

It wasn't the first time Dan had danced to the sting of Mike Royko's lash. In 1980, the anchorman had hopped a Chicago taxicab, heading for an interview with local literary icon Studs Terkel, but the cabbie couldn't find the house. A screamfest ensued and, according to the CBS star, the driver then held him hostage, speeding recklessly through the Windy City as he yelled for help out the window.

It was vintage Rather, once again. The CBS star filed a complaint with cops, but later dropped it. Royko savaged Dan casting him as "Mr. Big Shot" picking on a Little Guy.

In 1986, Dan made shocking news headlines yet again—and truly threw a scare into CBS. In a bizarre encounter, he was walking alone on New York's upper-crusty Park Avenue one early evening when two men in dark suits reportedly accosted him and demanded, "Kenneth, what's the frequency?" Rather responded, "I beg your pardon?" and one of the men smashed a fist into his face. The blow staggered the anchorman, who turned and ran into the foyer of a fancy apartment building. The two men raced after him, pummeling and kicking as they repeated their eerie mantra: "What's the frequency, Kenneth?" An outraged doorman kept yelling at them to stop, but the men paid no attention. After administering the beating, they strolled off unhurriedly.

It was an unsolved case, and it sent shock waves through the executive suites of CBS. Who were these men? The attack had none of the earmarks of a robbery, so why had they assaulted Dan? And who was Kenneth? It couldn't be a case of mistaken identity. Dan Rather was one of the best-known faces in America.

Did Dan have some deep, dark secret that was about to surface and erode his credibility?

For more than a decade, that mysterious attack cast a shadow over Dan's public persona. Comedians cracked jokes, writers referred to it in stories about Dan, and the rock group R.E.M. recorded a song called "What's the Frequency, Kenneth?" In another oddball twist, CBS *Late Show* host David Letterman persuaded the anchorman to appear on his show with the band . . . and join them on backup vocals. Then, as often happens with Dan Rather, the case took a truly weird turn. In early 1997, the *New York Daily News* trumpeted their scoop headlined:

"What's The Frequency? Rather I.D.'s '86 Mugger!"

TV critic Eric Mink wrote, "After more than 10 baffling years, CBS anchor Dan Rather has identified the man who beat him in a bizarre incident on Park Ave. The assailant is William Tager, the same man who fatally shot an NBC technician on the street outside the *Today* show studios in 1994."

Mink noted that Rather had examined photos of Tager supplied by the *Daily News* and confirmed: "There's no doubt in my mind that this is the person."

The story explained that Rather had been ribbed and ridiculed about the enduring mystery, with some doubting the anchorman's account. But the question that popped into every reader's mind was, "Just one man? Weren't there two?" Explained the *Daily News:* "Rather told police it was just his impression that the attacker was accompanied by another man. Only one person actually beat him. Rumors and industry gossip swirled after the attack, including suggestions that Rather had been beaten by the jealous husband of an alleged lover—and that he was losing his grip on reality."

Who was the man Dan Rather had now fingered as his mysterious attacker? William Tager, a six-foot-two, two-hundred-pound motorcycle dealer and textile merchant from North Carolina, had a history of alleged violence. He'd often told friends about hearing voices from the TV networks and claimed they were "after him."

In 1994, Tager came to New York and murdered an NBC-TV technician outside the *Today* show studios, using an automatic rifle. After cops arrested him, Tager told them "rays were coming on top of him and vibrations came out of the TV." He also insisted he'd attacked Rather in the 1986 incident, but law enforcement decided not to press charges because the statute of limitations had run out.

After the killing, Tager was examined at the request of prosecutors by Dr. Park Dietz, a forensic psychiatrist. Dr. Dietz told the *New York Times* that Tager—who's serving a twelve-and-a-half-to-twenty-five-year sentence for manslaughter—believed that the evening news was broadcasting messages directly at him. In the course of his examination, Dr. Dietz's curiosity was piqued by Tager's insistence that he had attacked Dan Rather. But was he telling the truth? Dr. Dietz eventually contacted the anchorman to see if his memories of the incident matched those of his alleged assailant. According to the doctor, Rather recalled details about the Park Avenue building that he'd fled into during the attack that exactly matched Tager's memories. Finally, Rather identified Tager from the *Daily News* photos.

Incredibly, Tager had confessed to Dr. Dietz that he'd contemplated doing even worse harm to the evening news anchor—his imagined tormentor. After identifying Tager, Rather said he was relieved that the matter had been resolved. "Everybody's had their say about what happened, and some have had fun with it. Now the facts are out. My biggest regret," Rather added, "is he wasn't caught before he killed somebody."

One final weird footnote: A woman who charged that Tager had repeatedly rammed her Volkswagen with his Jeep when she parked outside his North Carolina yarn business in 1988 said, "I was very afraid of him. He screamed at me that I was . . . a liberal."

Which, in the wake of Rathergate, is exactly what Dan's detractors are screaming.

Chapter 4

L*eft-wing devil!*"

"*Public Enemy No. 1!*"

And that's what vast right-wing conspiracy folks call Dan Rather when they're feeling *good!* But are all those right-wingers . . . right? Two questions must be answered before the Court empanels you on the Rathergate Trial jury:

1. Is Dan Rather a liberal?
2. Did he rush to air phony documents attacking right-wing Christian President George Bush because he is biased?

On Question 1: Dan denies, denies, denies he's a liberal, but . . . Dan is a liar. On Question 2: Let us consider more evidence before answering.

First, let's consider the "Dan is a liar" statement. It's bald and overly pejorative, perhaps—after all, he's not denying murder or heinous crimes—and I'll cop to sounding as overwrought as, well, Rush Limbaugh or L. Brent Bozell Jr. And let me state, for the record, that my opinion of party politics—based on my early years as a political reporter who loved the game—is that it's great fun for people who like to join things.

I never join things. I am a newspaperman, a journalist—an equal-opportunity basher. For a recent birthday my daughter gave me a card depicting a pompadoured punk sporting a ducktail cut and a greasy motorcycle jacket with the caption "My Dad . . . the Rebel!" Right on, little girl.

My point is, I'm not a right-winger adding to the millions of words written about Dan Rather's wild-eyed liberalism. But it's my opinion, based on considerable research into his writings and his attitudes, that Dan Rather's a knee-jerk leftie—whether it's honestly subconscious or not. If it's something subliminal, Dan, I recommend that you, as a dogged newsman who worries truth like a bone, sit down and peruse objectively your utterances and actions over the years. The following, I modestly suggest, might be a jumping-off point for you.

Let's hark back to the pasting Rather took for his incredibly aggressive, rude badgering of then-Vice President George Bush? In his book, *The Camera Never Blinks Twice*, Dan wrote in his own defense:

> Journalists of integrity ask questions. We don't come to conclusions before getting what can be considered reasonably honest answers. Especially when an interview subject is involved with allegations of serious wrongdoing in public office, it is the responsibility of an ethical journalist to ask direct questions—and keep on asking them until the subject answers, or until it is clear he refuses to answer.

Rather's crystal-clear declaration paints the familiar self-portrait that's always on exhibit. Is it real—or is it hogwash?

In 1999, Howard Kurtz, media critic for the *Washington Post*, interviewed Rather on CNN's *Reliable Sources* and asked why he'd been a pit bull with right-winger Bush, but a pussy-cat with impeached Oval Office adulterer Bill Clinton, the Mother of All Liberals. His evasive reply reveals that while he believes reporters should ask tough questions, answering them frankly is not a priority—where he's concerned.

> KURTZ: You were also very aggressive with Vice President Bush when you interviewed him on CBS during the Iran-Contra affair. But when you interviewed President Clinton a couple of months ago, after this long impeachment ordeal, you asked him such things as: "How is the First Family holding up?" "Did the past year have a moral?" "What can parents tell their children about this whole episode?" Why didn't you ask him, you know, "Mr. President, with all due respect, you put the country through a terrible ordeal, you lied to your friends and closest advisers, and how can anyone trust you again?" Were you pulling any punches?
>
> RATHER: No, I don't pull punches. I go into each interview thinking to myself, "How can I make this the best interview I've ever done, and how can I make this the best interview he's ever done? But the question is fair. First of all, he'd been asked a version of those questions at news conferences and other forums—that's number one. Number two, you know, I've learned that there are three things that every man at CBS News thinks he can do better than any other man: one is to judge a Miss

America contest, two is coach the Knicks, and three is to do big interviews. Everybody has their idea about how the interview should be done. I sized up the moment— the news moment, if you will—sized up President Clinton, and I thought the interview was as revealing as anything he had done.

Bravo, Dan! Talk about ducking a tough question. Here's the honest answer you should have given to Howard Kurtz: "Well, I guess you caught me with my bias unzipped, Howard. Ha, ha. I guess I've got to admit that my questions to President Clinton were softballs Larry King would envy. I didn't mean them to be, but I just get this warm glow when Bill's around. Why was I tougher on Bush than Clinton? I guess it's because I just don't like George Bush or what he stands for. But I like Bill Clinton a lot. I'd boil coffee on his campfire anytime. And I guess it shows, Howard."

The morning after Rather's softball soiree with Liberal-in-Chief Bill Clinton, the anchor sat in on *CBS This Morning* with host Harry Smith and raved on about his close encounter like a dewy-eyed schoolgirl: "He's a very good historian. Harry, I think if you had been in the room, any viewer-listener who had been in that room, would have been impressed with the breadth of his knowledge about Clint Eastwood and his new movie *Unforgiven,* Jack Nicholson's role in *A Few Good Men,* and then switched to a knowledgeable analysis of Arkansas's chances against North Carolina in the big basketball game tomorrow night."

Whoa, hoss! Hard-News Dan comin' off like one of them gushy, girly-man gossip columnists? Sounds like Mike Walker dishin' about—what's he call her?—hubba-hubba Angelina Jolie!

Now, before I'm accused of being rather biased, let me quote a man who's not merely one of Dan's good and true pals, he's racked up a rock-solid track record of saying exactly what he believes—even when it hurts. And usually, it hurts *him!* I'm referring to grizzled *60 Minutes* gadfly Andy Rooney, who in 2002 told Larry King on his CNN show: "I think Dan is transparently liberal. Now, he might not like to hear me say that. I always agree with him, too. . . . *But I think he should be more careful.*"

Whoa!

The italics are mine. Read those eight words again carefully. Marvel at a classic Rooney bombshell, one pithy phrase that speaks volumes. What this very experienced network TV professional is telling you, folks, is his longtime friend and colleague Dan Rather allows his liberal sympathies to affect his supposedly unbiased newscast.

That statement, coming as it does from a CBS staffer, is sheer dynamite. When I discovered, in researching this book, that Andy Rooney had passed that unequivocal judgment on the eight-hundred-pound gorilla of CBS News—on national TV, no less—my first thought was that everyone at Dan's network must have been lunching at Le Cirque and missed it. Further research uncovered the fact that, unfortunately for Andy Rooney, they had not. Andy secretly caught hell about his remark from CBS honchos—and apparently from Dan himself, as I'll explain further along.

Incredibly, Rooney's quote was barely noted by anyone

outside of CBS News. One newspaper mentioned it in passing, and everyone has forgotten it now. But can you imagine the furor if Rooney had uttered those words in the wake of Rathergate? A firestorm would have ensued. Why? Because the statement is unequivocal, open to only one interpretation.

When Andy Rooney says Dan Rather "should be more careful," he obviously isn't simply suggesting that the anchorman should chill on his political views when he's, say, knocking back bourbon-and-branch with the boys. No, folks, that was a no-spin statement. Andy Rooney believes that *CBS Evening News* anchorman Dan Rather is "transparently liberal"—what right-wingers call "a bleeding-heart"—and that he allows political bias to seep into his supposedly objective reportage.

Please note: If Rather considers the Texas loony who slipped him those phony Dubya/National Guard documents "unimpeachable," then Rooney, a CBS colleague, must rate somewhere north of the pope as a source.

Research reveals that volumes could be filled with all the right-wing rants leveled against Dan and his alleged left-wing bias. If you imagine Karl Rove leading all the imps of hell in a chorus of right-wing demon speak, you've got it. So, to shed calmer light on the question of Dan Rather's alleged left-wing bias, let's consider another fabled CBS News star's experience with him. This veteran newsman identifies Rather as a friend and colleague "whom I have worked with and genuinely liked for most of my adult life."

In his riveting *New York Times* bestseller *Bias,* Emmy-winning TV correspondent Bernard Goldberg relates the chilling tale of how his pal Rather whacked him—professionally, that is—after he penned a newspaper piece accusing the networks, and such "media elites" as Dan, Tom Brokaw, Peter Jennings, etc., of slanting the news leftward. Writing in the *Wall Street Journal* in 1999, Goldberg didn't mince words: "There are lots of reasons fewer people are watching network news, and one of them, I'm more convinced than ever, is that our viewers simply don't trust us. And for good reason. The old argument that *the networks and other 'media elites' have a liberal bias is so blatantly true that it's hardly worth discussing anymore.*"

Bada-*bing!*

Once again, the italics are mine—for emphasis. As for the "bada-bing," the *Sopranos* imagery is Bernard Goldberg's. Explaining his experience, he likens the mob known as the Media Elites to that close-knit group we loved to watch on HBO. After he opened his mouth about "the family business," how do you think what Goldberg calls the "News Mafia" reacted?

Fuhgeddaboudit!

Here's a guy who spent twenty-eight years as a news correspondent with one of the three big "families"—CBS News—and here's how he summed up the story, in his own words: "Bernie G opened his big mouth to the wrong people—and he got whacked!"

From the moment his *Wall Street Journal* piece about liberal bias in Big Media hit the street, Bernard Goldberg was a marked man. Today, he sleeps with the fishes—network news-wise, that is!—thanks to The Don. As the ex-CBS newsman explains it in *Bias:* "The Don in this case is actually The Dan. Dan Rather. *Capo di tutti news guys.* It's not generally known, but The Dan even speaks his own secret language, called Dan-ish . . . In Dan-ish, 'it's all my fault' means 'it's all your fault' . . . 'no problem' means big problem . . . and 'don't worry, amigo' means 'worry a lot, you unworthy piece of crap.'"

Goldberg extends his amusing gangland metaphor by adding that if CBS New were a prison, "100 percent of the vice presidents would be Dan's bitches."

Hilarity aside, the tale is tragic, and it affords outsiders a shocking look at the secretive, ruthless world of the Media Elite. It's a Halloween tour of the Byzantine labyrinth of newsroom hierarchies in which truth is too often lost or hijacked— by lying rogues like Jayson Blair of the *New York Times* and Jack Kelley of *USA Today*—or distorted by the sloth and bias of pompous cardboard cutouts who call themselves reporters.

I'll be naming names, so stick around. You ain't seen nothin' yet. But first, what happened to Bernard Goldberg when he blew the whistle on liberal bias in his own news organization?

"The Whacking of Bernie" began when the star correspondent, who'd been concerned by what he feared was a growing problem of politically slanted news, saw a CBS report that reeked of smart-ass liberal bias. A correspondent named Eric Engberg, "a longtime friend," began an on-air report about Republican presidential candidate Steve Forbes and his flat-tax proposal like this: "Steve Forbes pitches his flat-tax scheme as an economic elixir, good for everything that ails us."

In his *Wall Street Journal* piece, Goldberg pointed out that words like "scheme" and "elixir" are loaded, "conjuring up images of Dr. Feelgood selling worthless junk out of the back of his wagon." He went on to criticize Engberg for breaking a standard rule of journalism: If you're going to use an expert source to comment, identify the source's affiliation so the reader or viewer knows where they're coming from. For example, when Engberg allowed an economist from the Brookings Institution to ridicule Republican Forbes's flat-tax proposal, he failed to tip his audience that Brookings is a liberal think tank. In other words, his expert was a guy who might have had an ax to grind. Engberg was unprofessional in not pointing that out.

It's like identifying O. J. Simpson as a domestic-abuse expert who feels the problem is overblown—without pointing out that Mr. Simpson stabbed his wife to death.

Engberg wrapped up his news report with a steal from David Letterman, saying that "Forbes's Number One Wackiest Flat-Tax Promise" was the candidate's belief that it would give parents more time to spend with their children and each other. (Oh, yeah, that's a real wacky goal, dude.)

The final utterance in this blatantly biased comedy bit masquerading as objective news was: "The fact remains—the flat tax is a giant, untested theory. One economist suggested, before we put it in, we should test it out someplace . . . like Albania."

Oh? And which economist was that, Engberg? The liberal one you're using to make fair comment on the conservative's proposal?

But Bernie Goldberg got the last word in the *Wall Street Journal*—and it was devastating. Speaking of his very own CBS News, he wrote: "You'd have a better chance of getting the facts someplace else . . . like Albania."

Bada-*boom!*

The day before the *Journal* piece ran, Goldberg phoned

Rather to give him a heads-up about its content. And he recalls encountering The Dan—the man hiding behind that big TV smile, "the one who operates with the cool precision of a Mafia hit man, who kisses you on the cheek right before he puts a bullet through your eyeball. So when *that* Dan assured me, sounding more like The Godfather than The Anchorman, that 'Bernie, we were friends yesterday, we're friends today, and we'll be friends tomorrow'—I knew I was dead."

Of the dozen-odd books written by and about Dan Rather and CBS, Bernard Goldberg's *Bias* rips the lid off the Media Elite with the lusty savagery of a hyena cracking bones in his jaws. If his "The Don/The Dan" analogy horrifies while it cracks you up, you've no doubt ruminated over the same question that occurred to me: If CBS News truly cared about its viewers and wanted to constantly improve the quality of their news reports, why would they force out a star correspondent for venturing an informed opinion about how the news gets slanted?

It wasn't as if Goldberg had suggested CBS was broadcasting phony news. It's no shocker to anyone—much less viewers of TV or readers of periodicals, that a person's opinion can slip into the way they present things. We're only human, after all. And speaking of being human, I can't blame CBS News and Dan Rather for being annoyed that Bernie Goldberg didn't give them a real early warning about his piece. Most reporters give the subjects of a piece like that the opportunity to comment. Nonetheless, as you'll learn, the retaliation was brutal. The News Mafia could give the real Mafia lessons.

Here's one more item that's relevant to our armchair Trial of Dan Rather: the reaction to the *Wall Street Journal* piece that Goldberg got from CBS News president Andrew Heyward—who is, don't forget, one of the Rathergate principals under investigation by the so-called "independent" CBS panel. I put quote marks around *independent* because, like Dan Rather, I was trained to ask questions. My question is this: Seeing as how Heyward is one of the "suspects" under investigation, why the hell was he allowed to help choose the supposedly unbiased panel members who will pass judgment on him directly?

With respect, Mr. Heyward, answer *that* question!

After Goldberg's piece appeared in the *Journal* all those years ago, Andrew Heyward was apoplectic. In trying to calm his irate boss, Goldberg pointed out that he hadn't reported the fact that "even you, Andrew, have agreed with me about the liberal bias." Heyward, recalls Goldberg, immediately went ballistic.

"That would have been like raping my wife and kidnapping my kids," he screamed.

Recalled Goldberg: "If there was an instant when I knew just how dark it would get, this was it."

Shades of Tony Soprano!

It would get a lot darker for Goldberg before it got light again. Even journalists may be surprised to read this cautionary tale about how he was vilified and savaged by his peers. It chronicles a dirty little secret: We in the press love blowing the whistle but react like thugs when someone blows the whistle on us. (Just wait for the screams you'll hear emanating from New York and D.C. when this little baby of mine hits the streets!)

In trying to justify his action, Goldberg penned two letters of explanation to his longtime friend and colleague, Dan we-were-friends-yesterday Rather. He even had the letters hand-delivered.

Dan never replied . . . never, ever spoke to him again.

When Goldberg called Eric Engberg to discuss his actions, the reporter listened, then said, "OK, Bernie, here's my response. You're full of s——." And he slammed down the phone on their friendship forever.

Now, none of this "baloney" about liberal bias that surfaced after Goldberg's article was NBC anchorman Tom Brokaw's business—or was it? Because Dan's arch-rival suddenly stuck his oar in and huffed that he judged it "inappropriate" for Goldberg to "go to a newspaper like the *Wall Street Journal* [and] attack your own organization."

Does that sound like someone whose ox just got gored?

It was no surprise that Bob Schieffer, chief Washington reporter for CBS News, chimed in with the party line and said of coworker Goldberg: "If this place is as ethically corrupt as he seems to think, I think he'd have no alternative but to resign."

Don't complain, quit! Great advice for us ballsy journalists, Bob. I remember watching Rather throw it to you on the *CBS Evening News* after describing you as a "hard-hitting" reporter. You then read a canned statement from the Democratic National Committee, or some such. One would need to cast a wide net to dredge up a finer specimen of *apparatchik journalisticus.*

To be fair, Brokaw & Company have a point when they question why Bernard Goldberg was naïve enough to think he could write an honest piece about the news business—his own organization included—and expect fair and unbiased reaction. Admittedly, it seems a bit disingenuous for a street-wise reporter not to expect a major reaction, particularly as he failed to inform anyone in advance. Yet Goldberg acted dazed when colleagues he'd known and worked with for years suddenly dumped him like a Laredo rattlesnake with bad sunburn.

Yee-hah!

Yep, them thar Media Elites figgered Tenderfoot Bernie had oughtta git him some hoss sense, 'cause it gits dang lonely out on the old news prairie when a feller ain't got a friend. And there couldn't be a better authority to quote on that point than The Dan himself, who told *People* magazine way back in 1977: "This is a vicious and competitive business, and any-body who forgets it does so at his peril."

It is worth noting that in the midst of Goldberg's vilifica-tion, irrepressible curmudgeon Andy Rooney wrote Goldberg the following note:

"Bernie: In the future, if you have any derogatory remarks to make about CBS News or one of your co-workers . . . I hope you'll do the same thing again."

Ballsy guy, that Rooney. Irish guy. Like me.

So Bernie Goldberg cut a deal, departed CBS News and wrote two books, *Bias* and *Arrogance.* In the latter, he reveals that while the Media Elite either missed or ignored Rooney's astounding statement on Larry King that Dan Rather is "transparently liberal," his CBS bosses slapped him right on the grill. In a syndicated newspaper column written shortly after his trip to the woodshed, Rooney admitted that "they thought I shouldn't have said it. In my own defense, I told a boss of mine that I thought if all the truth were known by everyone, it would be a better world. He scoffed."

Scoffed? Andy's boss—and that could only be CBS News president Andrew Heyward or *60 Minutes* producer Don Hewitt—scoffed at the idea of telling the truth. Think about it! These are the journalism decision-makers at CBS News, yet they reject the very principle of telling the truth, of reporting the news objectively. Not to belabor the obvious, but that helps to explain why Dan Rather was dead last in the evening news ratings for years, does it not?

Oh, and enquiring minds want to know, did Rather ever take Andy to task for the "transparently liberal" crack? When Bernard Goldberg asked that question, Andy replied, with no humor whatsoever: "I wouldn't want to lie to you about that."

So, can we take that as a "Yes," Andy?

"It just goes to show ya," as Rooney might say on *60 Minutes,* truth comes with a high price tag. Remember The Dan's warning: Don't let your mouth write a check your ass can't pay for!

Good advice, but in the wake of Rathergate and the parade of headline-making screw-ups committed by major news organizations in recent years, it's time for some fearless journalist to put his ass on the line and blow the whistle, loud and long. Somebody needs to rummage around in the underwear drawers of the Media Elites—and who better than me, the gossip editor of the *National Enquirer.* I'm a news insider operating outside that clubby Gotham clique—although I know things about those big boys (and girls) that won't be revealed in these pages.

What *will* be revealed? The secret behind the screw-ups and outright lies that occur in ivory-tower newsrooms far too often. Listen up, Media Elite! Stop sneering and pay attention! Here's all the news you *really* need to know.

Remember what The Dan told us: We're in a vicious business. Ignore Tabloid Boy at your peril. Enquiring minds want to know the source of this blight so pernicious that people trust the news far less now than they did just a year ago. It's time to expose insidious mismanagement that leads to inexcusable debacles like CBS News/Rathergate, *New York Times*/Jayson Blair, *USA Today*/Jack Kelley, CNN-*Time* magazine/Poison Gas Scandal, *Washington Post*/Janet Cooke, NBC/Exploding Bus, Mike Wallace/Secret Video Scandal, and on and on. . . .

But, Tabloid Boy, you ask, why does this story need to be told?

Ah, the Media Elite's favorite cop-out question, piously trotted out whenever some "renegade" reporter prints a story Big Media doesn't like, that it deems "tasteless"—or when the *National Enquirer* breaks a major scoop that catches them all flatfooted. I'm talking earth shakers like:

- Married presidential candidate Gary Hart caught cooking with hot dish Donna Rice.
- O. J. Simpson exposed as a liar after swearing he'd never owned Bruno Magli shoes that tracked his bloody footprints.
- Married Rev. Jesse Jackson fathering a secret love child with a church employee.

- Rush Limbaugh feeding his addiction to "hillbilly heroin" with illegal drug buys.
- The *National Enquirer* nailing the murderer of Bill Cosby's son by leading the LAPD into the woods where the killer's gun was buried.

True stories.

And truth—whether it's from the *New York Times,* the *National Enquirer,* or out of the mouths of babes—matters! Good journalism is good journalism, no matter who practices it. I broke the story of Michael Jackson's unnatural relationship with the thirteen-year-old boy who condemned him as a molester. No matter that Dan Rather, Tom Brokaw, and Peter Jennings sniff that about what they so arrogantly dismiss as "Hollywood news."

Crap! Or, as Dan always like to put it in cute Texas-speak, "Bullfeathers!"

Michael Jackson was—and is—a major world figure, as worthy of news coverage as, say, Trent Lott. Here are two dirty little secrets: (1) Dan Rather and CBS News could not—repeat, *not*—break the investigative stories that are a hallmark of the *Enquirer,* and of my own column, to be not so humble about it; (2) Dan & Company wouldn't dare poke a stick into the rat's nest of celebrity journalism because people like Tom Cruise and Jennifer Lopez and Julia Roberts are immensely rich, powerful people who love paying lawyers big bucks to fight news organizations.

And while we're on the subject, where *was* Dan when the

Enquirer unearthed the scandal of major political figure Jesse Jackson impregnating a staff member of his Rainbow Coalition? Why didn't the *CBS Evening News with Dan Rather* report that a paramour of a perennial presidential candidate/man of the cloth had given birth to a love child that Mrs. Reverend Jackson knew nothing about? More on that later, as we say in TV. But to reiterate about my Michael Jackson scoop: Events proved that the story was true, and the rules of good journalism were applied in unearthing it.

Now let's get at the truth of why America refuses to trust Big Media. What's the problem, and can it be fixed? *National Enquirer* readers—like most folks—are suckers for good, solid how-to stories packed with helpful, practical, problem-solving tips. I've worked long and hard on the following self-help, how-to piece just for you, Media Elites.

Read it, weep—then get to work. It's called: "How to Stamp Out Fear and Corruption in Your Newsrooms!"

Chapter 5

Racing to deadline on this treatise, I barely looked up during election night 2004 except to check in briefly on Dan Rather anchoring the CBS News coverage. At a glance, Dan looked pretty much like he always looks, so I went back to work.

But on the morning after the morning after America voted George Bush back into the White House, the *New York Post* ran a vicious editorial attacking the CBS anchorman. The *Post,* of course, is the mighty-righty tabloid newspaper owned by famously conservative media mogul Rupert Murdoch. Its columns routinely bulge with brutal broadsides against the likes of Rather and all the usual liberal suspects. But this blunt attack on the CBS anchor boggled even seasoned media watchers. It was ostentatiously signed, "The Editors." In other words, the *Post* was alerting its readers that the piece they were about to read was an *official* gangbang! It began:

Dan Rather was at his unctuous best as the election returns unfolded. . . . Defending CBS's refusal to call Ohio for President Bush—when NBC and Fox already had—Rather declared: 'We'd rather be last than be wrong.' With a straight face. Considering that he and CBS—in airing a transparently partisan hit on Bush based on forged documents—had established a new low in media bias, *that* took nerve.

The *Post* then launched WMD: "Or maybe he thought nobody would notice—which would mean that Rather's as much a moron as he is a hypocrite."

Moron?!

Savage language, even for the purple-prose *Post.* Yet it crystallized my sense of the noxious bile bubbling up through the detritus of words written, from every conceivable viewpoint, about Rathergate. There's no denying it: Many journalists of all persuasions are angry, to one degree or another, with Dan Rather. Consider the pejorative, perhaps even unfair, headline that ran on September 23, 2004, in *Editor & Publisher,* the dignified "bible" which proudly bills itself as "America's Oldest Journal Covering the Newspaper Industry." It read: "Thanks, Dan: Gallup Finds Trust in Media at New Low!"

E&P's story, in part:

In the wake of the CBS *60 Minutes* controversy, a new Gallup Poll finds the news media's credibility has declined significantly among the public.

The poll, taken Sept. 13–15 while the CBS report on President Bush's National Guard service was being questioned but before the network issued an apology, found that just 44% of Americans express confidence in the media's ability to report news stories accurately and fairly.

"This is a significant drop from one year ago," Gallup reports, "when 54% of Americans expressed a great deal or fair amount of confidence in the media. The latest result is particularly striking because this figure had previously been very stable—fluctuating only between 51% and 55% from 1997–2003."

Whoa! America distrusts the press more than ever—and it's "Thanks, Dan"?

With that headline, venerable *E&P* is apparently laying the sole blame for this dramatic nose-dive on the CBS News anchorman. Let's look at *E&P*'s support for this damning charge.

"Clearly, something new has happened to shake public confidence in the media," Gallup reports, "but whether that 'something' is the recent CBS News controversy *is a matter of speculation.*"

The italics are mine, just to emphasize that there appears to be no justification for the "Thanks, Dan" headline. I mean, come on, *E&P!* You're only slamming The Dan because you're pissed off at him. Yet, why not? Many journalists have jumped on that bandwagon, so don't be ashamed, *E&P,* to admit your hissy fit. But why pussyfoot with an unsupported headline that clearly trumpets that you're damning Dan for our plummeting popularity. I mean, why hang back? Kick some ass, boys! Own up to your animus with hard-hitting editorial peroration that amplifies your stealth-bomb headline. In for a penny, in for a pound, no?

Frankly, after decades of perusing *E&P,* I must admit the snarky "Thanks, Dan!" headline surprised and amused me— emotional responses never before stirred by that sober-sided journal. But come on, *E&P!* It's not your style to run a head-line the story does not support. Gallup states quite unequivo-cally that it's "a matter of speculation" whether Rathergate triggered this new and sudden decline in the public's trust of the media.

Yet I must admit, your headline felt . . . right, somehow. A tad unfair and rather biased, perhaps, but what the hell! You're only human. And even though the Gallup folks don't actually *blame* Dan, they're the ones who led the elephant into the room—they clearly consider him at least a possible cul-prit. Your "Thanks, Dan" headline simply warns us of the beast's presence. Let me congratulate you on your newfound feistiness, *E&P,* and on how unerringly your saucy headline sums up the festering anger resonating in the written and spoken comments of countless journalists who've weighed in on Rathergate. The anger is not unanimous, of course—when does the press agree *en masse* about anything? Yet the feeling's out there: Dan may not be single-handedly responsible for journalists ranking below lawyers and dentists, but he surely helped dig the ditch we stand in today. So it's more than "Thanks, Dan." It's, "Screw you, Dan! Thanks a lot!"

Why are my fellow newsies so angry, Dan might ask?

Perhaps because you're so damned pompous, Dan, con-stantly evoking the fabled names of the now tin-roofed "Tiffany Network"—Cronkite, Eric Sevaried, Edward R. Murrow. Veteran newsman and media critic Sander Vanocur put it like this: "It drives me up the wall when I hear people at CBS evoking the name of Murrow. Most of them couldn't carry his typewriter. CBS is now like a cult."

A *cult?*

Like the Moonies? Or the Branch Davidians?

So before this is over, perhaps it'll be another Waco—Stonewall Dan hunkered down inside Black Rock with acolytes Heyward, Howard, Springer, Moonves, et al., as helicopters disgorge rappelling SWAT teams and a police bullhorn bellows ultimatums.

"Step away from the typewriters. *Now!* That means you, Mr. Rather. We will open fire on the count of three if you do not *step away from the typewriter!*"

In *National Review,* Jonah Goldberg writes: "Across the media universe the questions pour out: Why is Dan Rather doing this to himself? Why does he drag this out? Why won't he just come clean? Why would he let this happen in the first place? Why is CBS standing by him? Why . . . why . . . why?"

Why are your fellow newsies so mad, Dan?

Look, pal, it's not just that you got the story wrong. We've all been there. Every good, aggressive reporter has blown a story. But you're one of the most recognized practitioners of our craft. You should be handling this better. Your smug, banty-rooster hubris plays right into the stereotypical image that infuriates your right-wing detractors. And it makes average folks suspect that the press not only gets it wrong a lot, but we're too damned self-righteous to admit it and set the record straight when we do. Hard-ass stonewalling and self-serving protestation further convince the American people that they simply cannot count on us to deliver news they can trust.

It's not the CBS News screw-up that angers journalists. We're all too aware of our ingrained fear that we'll be the next to get a story wrong. It's the "There, but for the grace of God, go I" factor. The way I read it, the anger boils down to this: It's one thing to make an honest mistake. It's quite another to fast-track a scandal based on amateurishly forged documents—knowing you could sink a sitting president at election time—then stonewall and spin when you're exposed, endlessly and ungraciously attacking "partisan forces" that include your own colleagues, until you're finally forced to apologize grudgingly.

Worse, it's downright arrogant and insulting to follow that fiasco by sitting comfy in your $10 million anchor chair and uttering smug paeans to your lofty journalistic standards—a gross canard that the *New York* Post rightly used as cannon fodder—while trolling for cheap laughs with your tired corn-pone shtick, like these hee-haws you spouted on election night 2004:

"This race is humming along like Ray Charles."

"We don't know whether to wind a watch or bark at the moon."

"The presidential race is swinging like Count Basie."

"In the southern states, they beat Kerry like a rented mule."

"Don't taunt the alligator till you cross the creek."

"This race is hotter than the devil's anvil."

"John Kerry has a lead as thin as turnip soup."

"This race is hotter than a Times Square Rolex."

And Dan's perennial favorite, uttered with no context at all: "If a frog had side pockets, he'd carry a handgun."

It's not that anyone expected Dan Rather to burst into tears during his election night coverage, even considering the cloud he was under in the wake of Rathergate. But there was a feeling that he could have soft-pedaled all that forced, overly cute and patronizing Texas talk, at the very least. Somebody wasn't thinking of the viewer. Or does somebody think the viewer is stupid?

Just before the presidential elections, Bill O'Reilly conducted a fascinating interview with Rather's famed CBS colleague and titular boss Don Hewitt. Hewitt was amazingly frank about the aura of disgrace hanging in the air. He went right to the heart of it.

> HEWITT: But here's the problem . . . do you put him on the air election night with the cloud hanging over him?
> O'REILLY: Would you?
> HEWITT: Oh, boy, that's an agonizing. . . . I'm glad I don't have to make that decision.

In the wake of the *New York Post's* vitriolic attack on Rather's stubborn reluctance to concede Ohio to President Bush, other observers were shocked when the CBS anchorman dressed down *60 Minutes* colleague Ed Bradley when he tried to explain—using numbers a child could understand—that Kerry could not win the state.

Rather's face took on that congealed look that suggests he's reaching for the sidearm you know he's got stashed under the desk, and huffed that Bradley "doesn't have a math degree." Quietly, but emphatically, Bradley—looking not the least bit amused at this dressing down—replied, "I used to teach mathematics."

Bada-bing! *Bang!* Take that, pardner!

Perhaps now would be a good time to repeat the epigraph

that led off this book, and to explain the mysterious attribution I attached to it:

> If a rooster squawks, don't be too quick to strangle him. He might be trying to tell you something.
>
> —DAN RATHER (?)

Nope! Dan Rather never said that. I did. Hence, the question mark. As it happens, that faux-Dan quotation popped out of my mouth over dinner at a swanky Beverly Hills hotel just after Rathergate. It was my ad-lib reaction when the publisher proposed that I write this book. I blurted: "If a rooster squawks, don't be too quick to strangle him. He might be trying to tell you something!"

Publisher David Dunham and editor Joel Miller chuckled and said something like, "Classic Dan Rather . . . I think I've heard him say that one." No, I rejoined, Dan never said that. But he should have—it would have served as an internal warning against his own overwhelming hubris! Dan just didn't listen when expert "roosters" hired by CBS News warned him that . . . *squawk!* . . . those George Bush/National Guard documents look wonky. And when his story hit the streets, Dan ducked a veritable flock of roosters that flew in his face . . . *squawk!* . . . those "pajama-clad" bloggers he despises so much, and even his own colleagues in the press . . . *squawk!* . . . all of them squawking to wake Dan Rather to the glaring evidence that his Bush-bashing documents were amateurish forgeries.

Squawk! SQUAWK!!

Sadly, Dan was not able to draw upon the wisdom inherent

in my Texas-style, circle-the-wagons exhortation to heed his inner horse sense. Nope, Dan moved on Dubya quicker than a rattlesnake crossing a hot rock! He up and strangled every dang one of them pesky roosters, without heeding what in tarnation they were squawking about!

While we're in down-home mode, here's something else enquiring minds want to know: What's the deal with all this "Dan Rather: Cowpoke" crappola? Yew ain't no cowboy, hoss! You grew up on the concrete prairies of Houston's inner city. With respect, answer *these* questions! Has Dan Rather even owned a horse? Or ridden one? Or owned a pickup truck? Has Dan Rather ever driven—or ridden in—an eighteen-wheeler? Hell, I'm a dang sight more of a cowboy, hoss. Owned and bred horses, trotted them out in show-ring competition, and 380 horses gallop under the hood of my Ford Lightning SVT pickup truck. It's super-charged!

Yee-hah!

But don't dump your dang Danisms on my say-so. Nobody begrudges you, Bubba! If you think they enhance your down-homey appeal, knock yourself out. Hell, if I was hauling down ten million bucks a year, I might try bonding with the commoners by dredging up folksy sayings reminiscent of my New England roots. Like:

"Bush comes off like cod trying to be halibut!"

"Kerry bogged down like a trawler in a seaweed patch!"

"This race is tighter than Ted Kennedy's shorts!"

On second thought, maybe this shtick only works for Texas.

One last observation on Danisms: I remember seeing Rather on a TV show where the host asked him to come up with a few fresh ones. The star anchorman stumbled a bit, then ad-libbed a couple that came off a trifle lame. Dan, it's no secret that those back-country bon mots are written for you, logged in the teleprompter and rehearsed. Not that there's anything wrong with that! But wouldn't it be wise to commit a handful to memory for those teleprompterless personal appearances?

As for Dan Rather's CBS News hoedown on election night 2004, this was one ratings race that was *not* tighter than Willie Nelson's headband. Statistics showed that the Big Three networks have lost millions of viewers since the last presidential election—and this time around, *The CBS News with Dan Rather* came in dead last.

Question is, was it due to the Rathergate fallout?

CBS placed a distant third behind NBC and ABC. Incredibly, Fox News Channel—considered a joke when it cranked up in 1996—netted 8.1 million viewers to CBS's 9.5 million.

And now, let's leave the bias question and move forward to the Trial of Dan Rather. But first, as they say in TV . . .

A far more serious problem has shaken major-league media organizations—the *New York Times, USA Today,* CNN, NBC, the *Washington Post,* and others. It sounds melodramatic, but fear and corruption is rampant in too many newsrooms. Before we can stamp out these evils, we need to identify exactly how they lead to distrust of the media. For those who are not members of the press, let me define journalistic fraud. It includes:

Plagiarism: You cannot steal another person's written words. You can be inspired by them, you can paraphrase them, you can even quote someone's work at reasonable length—it's called "fair use" in our business—but you must credit your source.

Fabrication: Lying, or making stories up out of whole cloth, is the deadliest sin. Pros use terms like "piping a story" or "lifting quotes"—the latter meaning sneaking an interviewee's quote from another reporter's story and pasting it into your own piped pastiche. Fabrication includes concocting events that never occurred, inventing quotes that were never uttered or stealing them from another publication, or—as we'll observe while analyzing the real-life cases of journalistic fraud that follow—actually giving birth to a fictitious person. Lesser degrees of fabrication that qualify as fraud also include exaggerating acts or utterances, altering a person's quotes unfairly, or stage-managing an event to tweak it with phony drama.

In any well-run newsroom, experienced editors are vigilant in vetting reporters' stories for errors, inadvertent or fabricated. The factor called human error inevitably occurs under deadline pressure, although a ticking clock should never be a convenient excuse for sloppiness. Fabrication is an evil that slithers, silent and undetected, into chaotic newsrooms when editors and reporters subordinate the job of recording facts to the never-ending need for blockbuster stories that will snag readers or ratings.

News is a business. Make no mistake about it. It's run by businessmen who bankroll the editorial budget but keep a cold eye on the bottom line. Occasionally, the bottom line wipes out the front lines—the foot soldiers out there fighting to get the news. That's what Laurence Tisch did to CBS. Made a hell of a lot of money, though. Tiffany schmiffany, right, Larry?

Owners demand that editors fill the paper or newscast with stories that sell. The editors put the heat on reporters, directing them toward events and trends that will make good copy. That's all fine. It's a pressure-cooker business, and most people who gravitate to news can handle it and often thrive on it, but . . .

Remember that sarcastic newsroom jibe a few pages back? *Don't let the facts stand in the way of a good story.* When editors who aren't good leaders relentlessly breathe dragon fire at reporters, the pressure—real or imagined—can create an unhealthy atmosphere in which facts get jazzed up or even invented. News is a deadline environment. It's called "news" because it's "new." It's a perishable commodity. You rush it to the marketplace fast or it starts to stink. Compare Reporters A & B in these scenarios:

EDITOR: (Picks up ringing newsroom phone) Yeah?
REPORTER A: Boss, the First Lady's pregnant!
EDITOR: *Wow!* I'll hold page one . . . file your copy. Great job!

Or . . .

EDITOR: (Grabs phone) Yeah?
REPORTER B: Boss, the First Lady's pregnant!
EDITOR: *Duh!* It went page-one an hour ago . . . buh-bye!

So, which reporter would you rather be? That's how it starts, news fans, with the feeling that you must scoop . . . or die! We'll soon touch on all these points as we relate some woeful, woeful tales.

Chapter 6

Her name was Janet Cooke. A beautiful young African-American woman of twenty-five, she'd graduated from Ohio's University of Toledo, worked in local TV and newspapers, and showed some talent. She'd set her sights on the big time, the *Washington Post*, but knew she didn't have the background to crack it. So she sat down at her typewriter and fabricated a dream resume: Phi Beta Kappa from Vassar, master's in literature, fluency in two foreign languages, TV experience, a writing award at the Toledo *Blade*, membership in the National Association of Black Journalists, etc.

"My goal," she confessed later to an interviewer, "was to create Supernigger."

Legendary *Post* editor Ben Bradlee was impressed. He passed the letter to another legendary figure, *Post* Metro Editor Bob Woodward, enthusing that Janet Cooke should be hired before the *New York Times* or the TV networks snapped her up. Incredibly, the *Post* did not check her credentials. She was hired—and just nine months later embroiled her paper in a journalistic scandal that made worldwide headlines. It started when Cooke wrote a heart-tugging tale about an eight-year-old African-American heroin junkie who lived in the ghetto of Washington, D.C. Her story created a sensation

and she won a Pulitzer Prize. But after a massive citywide police search failed to turn up her pathetic child addict, Cooke finally admitted that "Jimmy" had never existed. The Littlest Junkie was a figment of her fertile imagination.

A rank newsroom beginner had pulled the wool over the eyes of senior editors of the respected *Washington Post*— which then suffered the humiliation of shamefacedly returning Cooke's Pulitzer Prize.

Janet Cooke was fired, never worked in journalism again, and that's the bare bones of the scandal. But the details of this cautionary tale illustrate how fear corrupts integrity in newsrooms. Writer Mike Sager, who worked at the *Post* with Janet Cooke and was briefly her boyfriend, tracked her down sixteen years after the shocking incident and conducted a fascinating, in-depth interview that was published by *GQ* magazine. The picture that emerged in a piece that was soul-baring for Sager as well as his subject reveals the sometimes-unbearable pressure that hard-driving, overzealous news executives impose on reporters who can't summon the courage to stand up and say: *I'm doing the best I can, and if that's not enough, screw you!*

In his *GQ* story, Sager immediately tried to answer the first, most obvious question: Was Janet Cooke simply a liar who cynically concocted a sensational story to advance her career? After all, she'd fabricated her resume, hadn't she? And in filling Sager in on her background and upbringing, she freely admitted that, as the daughter of an almost unbelievably overbearing father, she and her mother and sisters became skilled in the art of telling lies to avoid confrontation. It was how they survived under a cold, rigid patriarch who ran their upper middle-class household with an iron fist, never allowing his daughters to leave the house except to attend school—forbidding them to invite friends into their home. Not surprisingly, Janet Cooke suffered from low self-esteem and had become adept at telling lies to extricate herself from difficult situations. Sager recalls that during their brief romantic relationship, he had often caught her lying and that eventually drove them apart.

Sager interviewed one of Janet Cooke's editors, an African-American woman long-since retired from the *Post*. Her unvarnished comments go a long way toward explaining how a young journalist who'd exhibited talent and drive suddenly committed the worst sin in our business—making up a story completely unfounded in fact.

She freely acknowledged that she hadn't liked the neophyte reporter right from the get-go because she displayed "a whole lot of glamour and flash, as opposed to substance." She said that when she'd conveyed this criticism to her young charge, Cooke asked, "What about my work?" The former editor recalled that she told the eager-to-please rookie: "It's fine, great. But you need to remember two things. First, no matter how good your last story was, people around here want to know, 'What are you going to do for me today?' Second, no matter how good a writer you think you are, you're nothing without me. I've made you what you are, honey pie. I can unmake you just as fast."

Sound like a healthy newsroom? Here's a young reporter being told: Your mission is not to serve the readers of this newspaper—it's to serve me! *Always think of the reader?* Hell, no, girl—you better be thinkin' about me!

The implicit threats and abuse in that statement are a text-book example of how not to train a journalist. Being tough is one thing; creating a bullying bureaucracy is quite another. There is nothing wrong with being tough and saying something businesslike, such as, "Deliver what I want and you'll be going places fast." Telling someone, "You're nothing without me" is dumb. It diminishes you. It reveals that you don't possess the natural confidence of a leader. Ruling by fear reveals your own fatal flaw—insecurity.

Now, as any fan of Shakespearean tragedy can see, the stage was set. But how did the *Washington Post's* nightmare come to pass? What started Janet Cooke down the road to worldwide notoriety as the poster child for journalistic fraud? It all began when she was out on one of her first assignments, interviewing staffers at Howard University's drug-abuse program. The fledgling reporter got excited when one of them mentioned that an eight-year-old boy was being treated for heroin abuse at a facility, but she played it cool. She fished for a name, but the staff clammed up and she got nowhere.

Back at the newsroom, according to Sager, Cooke told a senior editor what she'd heard and he enthused: "That's a f—ing front-page story. You've got to find that kid." But after eight weeks of frantic searching, Cooke was batting zip. No one could lead her to the alleged child addict. One drug administrator she begged to help her finally hinted there might be such a kid, but refused to name him. The senior editor who'd gotten so excited about Cooke's kiddie addict story idea became frustrated. He went to the paper's managing editor and requested a relaxation of the paper's usual standards regarding the identification of sources. The managing editor tried to help break the logjam by ruling that the administrator could be offered total anonymity for leading Cooke to the kid. No one's name—not the boy, or anyone helping Cooke—needed to be divulged to *Washington Post* editors.

It was better than a free pass to Disneyland. It meant that the integrity of the story now rested solely with Cooke. She'd been awarded a license to kill—and her victim would be the truth. The decision by the *Post's* top editors to confer such privileged status on a rookie reporter was ludicrous, a dereliction of their duty to the newspaper and its readers. Why did it happen? Let me repeat that journalistic homily I mentioned earlier: *Never fall in love with a story . . . there's always a better one coming along right behind it.* Every journalist knows the excitement that boils inside when you're hanging onto a hot story by your fingernails, fighting deadline pressure and the nagging fear that the competition's breathing down your neck. But there was no such deadline pressure on this story. And no competitor had heard of the holy grail child who'd come to be known as "Jimmy." The only person who truly believed he existed couldn't even find him. So what was the big rush?

Experience teaches a journalist to take a breath before you commit, to slow down and go over every angle again. Remember that look-before-you-leap analogy: *Every time you publish, you're jumping off a cliff . . . so make sure it's a bungee jump.* Just for good measure (please pardon the fast-approaching play on words) here's another of my newsroom homilies:

Check twice, publish once.

It's based on an old saw my dad drilled into me as he patiently imparted the art of woodworking—and we've all heard it before—measure twice, cut once.

So why didn't these editors chill and tell Cooke she'd have to keep looking for that elusive kid? And once she found him, they'd need solid proof that he really was a kid junkie. The decision should have been: No kid, no story! It's that simple. To put it in a context, I've worked for the *National Enquirer* for about twenty-five years. I'm no rookie. But if I proposed running a story about a tiny child being forced by his mom's drug-dealing boyfriend to take illegal heroin shots and told my editors that I would *not* produce the boy, they'd holler for a straitjacket. Let me repeat: No Jimmy, no story! That's the inflexible, never-breached *Enquirer* standard. I challenge any competent editor in journalism to stand up in debate and argue against that standard. Yet a senior editor and the managing editor of the *Post* fell head-over-heels in love with Janet's story, acting like giddy groupies—even though no shred of evidence had surfaced after eight weeks of work.

Common sense should have triggered someone's BS detector. But it didn't, because love is a powerful emotion. This was a hot story. And attractive, sexy Janet's own charms had apparently come somewhat into play, according to Sager in *GQ*. She was a rising star. Ben Bradlee and Bob Woodward had rushed to hire her, gushed about her potential—and they often dropped by her desk to hear her throaty chuckle and salacious jibes. Bradlee would puff out his chest and flirt with her in French. Woodward would just gawk. And Janet's "in" with the paper's most powerful editors wasn't lost on the staff. So basically, some very smart people just went gaga and told themselves: so what if we allow her to write a page-one story on her unsupported word? It's a huge story, isn't it? Well, sure, it does kinda exploit a child, but . . . what the hell, let's find the kid first!

Now the stage lights dimmed, the climactic moment approached. But what actually drove Janet Cooke to the extreme of inventing an eight-year-old heroin junkie? She could have dumped the idea. But now she was feeling the heat. It's mighty seductive when powerful editors bat their eyes and promise a page-one byline if you'll just bring them a blockbuster. They had bent over backward to bend the rules, so Janet was feeling the pressure. She'd hoped for a breakthrough after the editors authorized the offer of anonymity to the drug administrator who'd hinted Jimmy really existed. But when she approached him again, he suddenly stopped taking her calls. Janet went to her own editor, the woman directly in charge, and in a moment of despair *admitted she didn't think she'd ever find the boy.*

The italics are for emphasis. Because the response Janet Cooke got after that heartfelt confession was not only shockingly dismissive, it sounded like a green light: Get phony or get out. "Well, find another boy," her editor snapped. "It's make-or-break, girlfriend."

How's *that* for turning up the heat!

Another of my oft-repeated homilies for editors is:

Never put a reporter's job on the line when you demand a story—desperation breeds imagination.

A good editor would have asked the reporter: "Do you think this kid really exists? Or is someone just bulls—ing, the way people do? If you think it's a phony, dump it. You'll come up with something else."

A good editor would have suggested tips on tracking hard-to-find subjects, based on his or her experience. And a good editor—especially one who'd sized up a reporter as "all flash and no substance," a flake with low credibility—would not have let such a sensational story fly. But fly it did, written so achingly, so emotionally by the talented Janet Cooke.

"Jimmy is eight years old and a third-generation heroin addict, a precocious little boy with sandy hair, velvety brown eyes and needle marks freckling the baby-smooth skin of his thin brown arms. . . . There is an almost cherubic expression on his small, round face as he talks about life—clothes, money, the Baltimore Orioles."

The story is skillfully paced, describing in excruciating detail the moment Janet Cooke "witnesses" the drug-dealer boyfriend of Jimmy's mother administer the child's heroin shot.

"He grabs Jimmy's left arm just above the elbow, his massive hand tightly encircling the child's small limb. The needle slides into the boy's soft skin like a straw pushed into the center of a freshly baked cake. Liquid ebbs out of the syringe, replaced by bright red blood. The blood is then re-injected into the child. 'Pretty soon, man,' Ron says, 'you got to learn how to do this for yourself.'"

The writing talent is unmistakable. The journalistic crime, unforgivable. Incredibly, Cooke got away with it. Instead of red flags, her editors threw her high-fives. The presses rolled, the story hit the street, and the *Washington Post* switchboard, in the words of one report, "lit up like a space-launch control room." Outraged readers were insisting that the *Post* shouldn't write about little Jimmy then callously ignore his plight—the paper should badger authorities to find the boy and rescue him from a life of horror. It was a twist Cooke hadn't expected. Her bombshell had created a firestorm. Unlike so many newspaper stories, this one didn't just fade away as birdcage liner. Washington, D.C., Mayor Marion Barry galvanized a massive police search for little Jimmy. He even announced at one point that officials had discovered the kid's identity and learned that he was actually getting treatment. It wasn't true. The mayor later withdrew the statement.

Despite the intensive search efforts, Little Jimmy was nowhere to be found. Police finally labeled the story a hoax. At the *Post,* some in the newsroom were finally becoming skeptical, but not the higher-ups. Believers included Metro Editor Bob Woodward, who'd signed off on Cooke's piece. Said Woodward: "The story was so well written and tied together that my alarm bells simply didn't go off. My skepticism left me."

The amazing hoopla over her story had Cooke frazzled. Keeping her guilty secret became a painful, lonely burden. Sager reported that as months went by, her nervousness escalated. She began to drink, take prescription drugs. She developed insomnia, got frightened when the doorbell rang. Unable to confide in anyone, she'd complain that she wasn't feeling well, only to be told by her mother and others: You should feel great. You're under consideration for a Pulitzer Prize.

Seven months after her front-page story, the Pulitzers were announced—and all hell broke loose at the *Washington Post.* Wire service reports of Janet Cooke's Pulitzer bio had run in newspapers across the nation, and it differed from the bios she'd given the Toledo Blade and the *Post.* For the Pulitzer bio, Cooke had added two more languages, six more writing awards, and a year at the Sorbonne. After hours of grilling by Ben Bradlee, Woodward, and others, she finally admitted: "There is no Jimmy. . . . It was a fabrication. I want to give the prize back."

All those years later, Sager wrote in his *GQ* piece, the editor in charge of Cooke believes that winning a Pulitzer "was not her endgame. She just wanted to get . . . away from me."

That statement goes unerringly to the core of my subjective sense of what triggered this astounding debacle. Janet Cooke caused the biggest scandal in the history of journalism. But she had enablers called "editors" who didn't fulfill their job description. She got what she deserved, but, with respect, answer the question: Should hers have been the only head to roll?

Chapter 7

It's early November as I write this. George Bush, despite Dan Rather, has been elected to a second term as president. A portentous headline in today's *Wall Street Journal* puts pressure on me to write faster—that is, if I want to go down in history as the Rather-inspired prophet who first sighted *this* fiery script written in the sky:

Smite fear and corruption from thy newsrooms, lest ye be doomed!

Yea and verily, there are signs and portents that the Media Elites, smug and insular in their Mordoresque towers, are finally beginning to sense that the hobbits grow restless in the shires. Swift on the heels of *Editor & Publisher* blaming Dan Rather for the recent plummet in news media approval, the *Wall Street Journal* trumpets dire warnings of fire on the plain. The headline: "How Dan Rather and Media Kings Lost Their Crowns!"

Daniel Henninger writes,

In the Information Age, authority is a priceless franchise. But it is this franchise that Big Media, incredibly, has just thrown away. It did so by choosing to go into overt opposition to one party's candidate, a sitting president. It stooped to conquer. The prominent case studies here are Dan Rather's failed National Guard story on CBS and the front page the past year of the *New York Times*.

Look on the bright side, Dan. The *Times* got some of the blame. Once again, the *Journal* cites the Gallup Poll that "reported that public belief in the media's ability to report news accurately and fairly had fallen to 44 percent—what Gallup called a significant drop from 54 percent just a year ago. . . . Big Media chose precisely the wrong moment to give itself over to an apparent compulsion to overthrow the Bush presidency."

So, it's that bias thing again. Everybody's talking about it since Dan jumped the shark. But notice that no one bursts forth with any workable solution to the problem. Surprise, surprise! That's because no journalist I know believes there's a prayer in hell or heaven that bias in media can be eradicated. Overt slanting of news could be controlled somewhat if a media organization's owners issued no-nonsense orders to slam on the brakes—heavy-duty bias always starts at the top. But in practice, the effectiveness of a no-bias policy would depend on the vigilance and dedication of the newsroom gatekeepers.

And how do you stop more subtle colorations generated by self-righteous stuffed shirts who signal their opinion by the choice of an adjective, the raising of an eyebrow, the smart-aleck smirk? To these elitists, it's never "bias"—it's "doing the right thing." Tom Brokaw, Peter Jennings, and Dan Rather endlessly deny that Big Media slants news leftward, scoffing at the concerns of a viewing audience that grows steadily more sophisticated, more aware of how to judge news that journalists feed them.

Suddenly, though, The Public is not passive. They are deliberately erasing the influence of Tom, Peter, and Dan, tuning out in increasing numbers, dismissing the Big Three anchors as anachronisms. Why? Because, as the Gallup poll shows, there is more doubt than ever about "the media's ability to report the news accurately and fairly."

For a comment on that, let's open the microphone to Dan Rather, speaking on radio in a Denver interview: "Now respectfully, when you start talking about a liberal agenda and all the, quote, 'liberal bias' in the media, I quite frankly—and I say this respectfully but candidly to you—I don't know what you're talking about."

A classic stonewall by the master. Note how quickly he chokes off discussion by professing ignorance that such a question even exists. Respectfully and candidly, Dan, here's what we're talking about: Conservative critics and press pundits danced the "I told ya so" hoedown when the *Washington Post* revealed that supposedly unbiased newsman Dan Rather had delivered a keynote speech at a Democratic fundraiser in Texas, apparently at the behest of a politically active family member. Interviewed about the eye-opening incident by Geraldo Rivera on Fox TV, Rather admitted: "Well, it was certainly one of the dumbest mistakes I ever made. But as you know, Geraldo—and you and I have known each other for a long time—I can be as dumb as a sack full of hammers about a lot of things. And what I really hated about that, it was a dumb mistake. There's no defense, and those who want to criticize me for that, I'd have to say I think that's a valid criticism."

After the anchorman's forthright confession of a mistake in judgment, the furor faded. So often, it's not the sin, but how you handle it. If Dan Rather had faced up honestly to Rathergate, the stain on his career would fade over time. On the battlefield of journalism, you can survive being shot down for bias and inaccuracy. Suppressing truth gets you zipped into a body bag.

Choosing between bias and accuracy as *bete noirs* of public trust in the media, it seems obvious that accuracy is the broke thing that needs fixing fast. If news isn't right, it's useless; in which case, bias hardly matters. We've covered both issues so far in the Trial of Dan Rather, but let's get back to our primary premise—that the Media Elites need lessons in accuracy and newsroom management that can be learned from the example of the *National Enquirer.* And why am I chosen to lead this master class? If you've been paying attention, you there in the back of the room, you know that far too many newsrooms are ruled by . . . what? All together now . . .

"Fear . . . Fear . . . Fear!"

Very good, class. So if most journalists won't stand up to the fear permeating their own newsrooms, who among them would have the brass balls to write a book like this? Not many, trust me. And who can blame them? Taking on the Media Elites would be an instant career-killer for most mainstream journalists. Tom and Peter and Dan and all their elite News Mafia pals would have a sit-down, put the word out on the streets and . . . *fuhgeddaboudit!* But me? Me, they can't touch. I've got my own gang. And messing with my gang can get . . . messy. So, I'm a guy who tells it like it is, without fear or favor. And they know it. *Capisce?*

Okay, let's get back to school here. What I'm writing on the blackboard now is a rock 'em-sock 'em headline that ran not long ago on page one of a major newspaper: "Explosion, Then Arms and Legs Rain Down."

Talk about an I-gotta-read-it headline! And the story supporting it—in which a reporter describes witnessing an actual suicide bombing in Jerusalem—was riveting. It was chosen as a final contender for a major journalism award. That it didn't win first place turned out to be very good news for the editors of *USA Today*. Because if their star foreign correspondent, Jack Kelley, had won that coveted prize, they would have faced the humiliation of surrendering it, just as the Washington Post had. Even though it was spared that shame, there were worse horrors to come. Janet Cooke had been a bad dream. Jack Kelley was journalism's worst nightmare—the rogue reporter who makes up page one lies and gets away with it for years! If Cooke was a jaywalker, Kelley was a serial killer.

Jack Kelley, a good-looking, smooth-talking Irish-American your mother would trust. A solid, even zealous Christian who so inspired a college journalism student that she wrote a touching essay about the day he visited her campus on a speaking engagement and told her one-on-one: "I'm passionate about reporting the truth and passionate about being accurate and objective. You don't only have to be ethical in your reporting, you have to live by those ethics as well.

. . . I believe God sent me into journalism to make sure that people know the truth."

The young woman listened mesmerized as Kelley sneered at other news organizations such as CNN, saying much of their reporting was "an abomination to everything journalists should be doing." Kelley skewered Fox News, saying it "infuriates me and embarrasses me as an objective journalist. I can't watch Fox News. I can't." To drive home his message of tough, objective journalism, Kelley added: "Never trust anyone. . . . Check everything out and make sure you have sources on everything."

No wonder the wee lass nearly fainted as the great man treated her to his great thoughts. Here was a dashing foreign correspondent for *USA Today* who'd been everywhere, seen it all. He'd regaled eager lecture audiences with high-adventure tales of rescuing children and soldiers from death, standing within earshot of torture chambers in Cuba, discovering a secret notebook that contained written orders for genocide. And, in the story from Jerusalem, Jack Kelley recounted how he'd been sitting outside a café when a suicide bomber struck at a pizzeria just ninety feet away. Kelley, who was about to lunch with a friend, had his back to the massive explosion that suddenly rocked the street. He wrote:

"Three men, who had been eating pizza inside, were catapulted out of the chairs they had been sitting on. When they hit the ground, their heads separated from their bodies and rolled down the street."

Wow! Shades of Hildy Johnson. Here was swaggering Jack Kelley, buckled into his foreign correspondent's Burberry trench coat, reporting from the ground zero of terrorism. But if that sounds exciting, you should have seen Jack's story as he wrote it in the first draft turned in to editors. His original copy contained an even more horrifying image. Jack wrote that some of the decapitated heads had rolled down the street "with their eyes still blinking."

Now . . . let's test your journalism skills. Read the excerpt from Jack's story again carefully, starting with the headline. I'll wait . . .

Finished? Okay . . . before going on to the next paragraph, pretend you're my editor and I've just turned in that piece of copy to you. What questions, if any, would you want to ask me? This book is not an interactive book, of course, so you can't actually ask me questions, so let's do this instead: I'll be your proxy—an experienced editor at the National Enquirer. And I'll fire off the questions I'm sure you'd ask the reporter who'd filed the story above. Here we go:

- Your copy says you were ninety feet away from the pizzeria where the suicide bomber set off the explosion. Right?
- Is it correct that you had your back to the pizzeria?
- You say the explosion blew the three victims right out of their chairs, right?
- You're sure their heads were instantly separated from their bodies?
- Here's my final question: You were ninety feet away, back to the three victims. The bomb goes off. *Bang!* Your first instinct was to duck, right? You must have cringed

at that huge noise. So that took at least a split second. Right? Now you swing around toward the explosion, focus your eyes from ninety feet away, trying to see through smoke and flying debris. Right? So how could you possibly have reacted fast enough to swing around and observe—as you wrote it—their bodies hit the ground, decapitated? The bomb would have decapitated them and flung their bodies to the street instantaneously. Right?

- Would you agree your explanation of how you could have seen all this makes very little sense?
- If you couldn't have seen all this detail from ninety feet away, after swinging around to focus through the smoke and debris, how the *hell* could you have seen heads rolling—and I'm quoting your copy—"with their eyes still blinking"?

Did this dialogue take place between Jack Kelley and his editors at *USA Today*? My years of experience tell me that someone clearly had suspicions, because the phrase "with their eyes still blinking" never made it into the final story. Somebody chopped it. Which means an editor with the authority to delete a star correspondent's copy knew he was reading an outrageous lie. Another journalistic homily:

When in doubt, leave it out!

So some unknown editor on *USA Today*—or perhaps it was several editors—apparently used common sense. To illustrate, let's put aside the question of whether eyes could possibly blink after a head is decapitated and ask ourselves a question that requires a judgment call. Is it possible, from a distance of ninety feet, to observe eyes blinking in a head that's bouncing down a street? Again, it's a judgment call, but how would you come to a decision? Well, you'd probably pick out a spot about ninety feet away, visualize a human head and its relative size from that distance, then imagine how tiny the eyes would appear to be, and you'd conclude that Jack Kelley is a damn liar. Obviously, someone at USA Today reached that conclusion, and deleted his phony anecdote. Question is, why didn't that person use the same good judgment and blow the whistle on Kelley's whole story? You'll come to appreciate the relevance of this lengthy disquisition on tough editing when we bang down the opening gavel in the Trial of Dan Rather.

Now, what was actually true—and what was false—about Jack Kelley's account? *USA Today* conducted an intensive ten-week investigation of his work over many years. In the Jerusalem bombing story, investigators finally contacted an independent source who confirmed that Kelley had indeed been at the scene of the bombing—but he was quite certain that the reporter didn't arrive until minutes after it occurred.

So, had Kelley simply dramatized what was true by claiming he'd eye-witnessed the bouncing heads of three victims? Sadly, it was far worse than that. According to Israeli police and the religious Jews who collect body parts of terror victims, *no one* was decapitated.

In another dramatic flourish to his terrorist tale, Kelley had written of an incredible coincidence. He'd actually brushed by the suicide bomber just moments before the attack. Kelley claimed he discovered this right after the attack, when an Israeli cop pointed to the head of the suicide bomber lying on the ground and said, "You've killed us all, you bastard."

In a TV interview with CNN—the news organization he claimed to despise—Kelley said he looked down and knew it was the bomber because "there was [the] gentleman's head laying on the floor, and I could recognize him as the gentleman who I had saw!" Impossible, scoffed Israeli police spokesman Gil Kleiman. He says Kelley couldn't have seen the bomber's head—because both head and body had been blown straight up by the blast and stuck in a vent above the pizzeria ovens.

As a stone-cold liar, Kelley ruthlessly toyed with human emotion. He invented a Rabbi Moshe Aaron, who told of finding the hand of a little girl "splattered against a white Subaru parked outside the restaurant." The phantom Rabbi Moshe told Jack that the child was "probably 5 or 6, the same age as my daughter." This disgusting lie was exposed by Israeli authorities, who keep a roster of those collecting body parts for insurance purposes. They report that there was no Rabbi Moshe Aaron present on that day.

Jack Kelley told a young journalism student that God sent him into journalism to tell the truth. Question: Did Jack make up that story, too? Here was a man who claimed deep religious faith, but hark to the chilling tale of how his lies could have ruined the life of a Cuban woman who actually was kind enough to help him while he was on assignment in Cuba.

Yamilet Fernandez was a hostess at the Havana hotel where Kelley stayed. As he pumped her for information about life in

Cuba, Yamilet told him of her plans to relocate to America as a legal immigrant. Stealing that truth as a basis for the scurrilous lies that would follow, Kelley concocted a wild story of a woman he called "Yacqueline," who fled Cuba in a small boat with six refugees and her little son. Tragically, Kelley wrote, the boat sank and everyone died.

It was a complete lie. *USA Today* investigators found the woman alive, married and pregnant, living happily in America. And here Kelley's deception gets truly evil. He had snapped a photograph of Yamilet in Cuba and, unbeknownst to her, allowed it to be published with his USA Today story as the last image of a woman who had died fleeing oppressive Cuba. It was a staggering, ruthless betrayal of a friend and identity theft in its most heinous form. When Yamilet Fernandez learned all this from the *USA Today* investigators, she was horrified—knowing that if Cuban authorities had identified her from the photograph, she'd have been accused of helping a foreign journalist, fired from her job, and blocked from emigrating. Considering the evil labyrinth of paranoid Cuban politics, Yamilet could have suffered consequences even worse.

Once again, *USA Today* editors were asleep. In many of Kelley's stories, he proved over and over that he was a colorful liar—but not a smart one. Here's another of my little homilies, repeated to my reporters:

Checkable facts will kill you.

Roseanne Barr once publicly accused two *Enquirer* reporters of smashing holes in the wall of a house after she'd moved out of it in Los Angeles—a bizarre claim that, as our lawyers pointed out, made no sense at all. Roseanne's lawyers backed off fast when the *Enquirer* produced airline tickets, hotel receipts, etc., showing that both reporters had been thousands of miles from California at the time. (The real culprit was eventually fingered, and the motive finally made sense—it was an alleged third-party insurance scam.)

One more example of how checkable facts can kill you. A reporter I know suffered severe shock after publishing a story about a celebrity who supposedly got pie-eyed on a plane, a domestic flight. What a sobering experience for that reporter when the celeb's lawyers produced airline tickets, hotel receipts, etc., proving their client was in Europe at the time. Here's the point on checkable facts: Stories that are challenged as wrong often come down to a he-said-she-said standoff. Reporters rarely eyewitness cataclysmic events—a shooting, a fistfight, a suicide bombing, a movie star sleeping with a major politician—so we rely on sources to tell us what occurred. Remember, we're like ambulance chasers. We arrive after the accident and start asking, "What happened? Did you see it?"

So when a story is suddenly denied, the reporter's defense usually is, "I trust my source." But if checkable facts are wrong, so is your lying source. There's no he-said-she-said. If somebody can prove they were in Madrid on the day you reported them in Malibu, you're dead meat, just as Kelley would have been if he'd attempted his stupid "Our Man in Havana" fiction at the *National Enquirer*. Our maddeningly meticulous research department would have checked the checkable facts in his copy and informed his editor: There was no storm that could have caused "raging seas" on the night that the boat supposedly sank.

Let me hasten to assure you that the *Enquirer* is not infallible. But our research department, put in place decades ago after we paid big bucks to hire away *Time* magazine's best, absolutely *is* infallible. Or as near to it as I've ever seen. After some of the pitched battles I've had with them, they may be surprised to hear me heap on the praise, but I don't think so. Like most hard-nosed editors, when you tell me I'm wrong . . . well, you'd better be right. But at the end of the day, I'll love you for saving me from Wrong Story Hell.

Every time you publish, you're placing enormous trust in sources and your own reporter's integrity, but do not operate on blind faith. Check what can easily be checked. Be instantly suspicious if any immutable facts contradict the story. Doesn't sound difficult, does it? Yet it's a routine apparently ignored, on the evidence, by some of the mightiest Media Elite. The purpose of this treatise is not to praise the *Enquirer;* we do what we do and we do it carefully. Again, any news organization can get a story wrong, but when you're reporting that powerful people like Rush Limbaugh or Whitney Houston are law-breaking drug addicts, you'd better be right. Too often, the Media Elite have proven that they're wide open to journalistic fraud.

Another thought on those tricky checkable facts: Even in perfect 20-20 hindsight, I'm not at all certain I would have caught Kelley's other moronic error. His copy said the refugee's boat was "guided by the dim light of a crescent moon." As *USA Today* learned in its subsequent investigation of Jack Kelley, there was no moon at all at the time of the boat's alleged capsize. Oops!

Now, before we leave this evil idiot to roast in whatever hell he occupies today, let's examine another illustration of transparent stupidity a competent editor should have caught. Any journalist who's been around the block knows that an expense account definitely falls under the heading of checkable facts. Kelley apparently forgot that while on assignment in Pakistan, where he allegedly covered U.S. commandoes searching for Osama Bin Laden around Ghulam Khan, a wild and lawless area near the Afghanistan border.

After filing his usual load of "Dashing Jack's Adventures" crap, he turned in his expense account—with a $3,540 payment to the translator who guided him to Ghulam Khan. Here's where *USA Today* totally blew it! Any good editor knows that a reporter's expense account, read intelligently, will reveal exactly what they're *really* doing.

A perfect example is the notorious ex-*New York Times* reporter Jayson Blair, whose outrageously phony stories about the Maryland snipers were published in the *Times* and brought about the shocking resignations of both the executive and managing editors. So, here was another Janet Cooke, a fledgling reporter who pulled the wool over the eyes of the so-called "paper of record" in a decidedly clumsy manner. For example, he couldn't have kept up his deception had anyone bothered to look at his expense reports and apply simple common sense. While Jayson Blair was getting kudos for filing blockbuster stories from Maryland and Virginia, all his expense receipts showed beyond a shadow of a doubt that he was in New York City! The ancient joke in journalism is that expense reports are where you find the finest examples of creative writing. Perhaps, but you can't disguise where the expenses were paid.

Going back to Kelley's case, his expense record showed he could not have spent nearly four days in Ghulam Khan—a nine-hour ride from his luxury hotel. And on all but one day of his eleven-day stay at the Islamabad Marriot, his expense account revealed, Jack Kelley was enjoying the pleasures of room service.

There's more—so much more. But Jack Kelley is just a useful example of what the Dan Rather/CBS News documents case, the Jayson Blair/*New York Times* case, and others we'll touch on are revealing in all their stark horror: The Media Elite need basic lessons in journalism. Ethics, too—but that goes beyond the scope of this treatise. And lest we be accused of crying "wolf," here's the mind-blowing digest of what the *USA Today* investigators saw as the system flaws that let their killer wolf run free:

- A "virus of fear" infected staffers, who were suspicious of Kelley's stories but were too afraid of his perceived power with top editors because he was "a golden boy" and "was seen as an untouchable." That made the staff "enablers for the fraud Jack Kelley produced."
- The paper's editing system—its policies, rules, guidelines—"should have raised dark shadows of doubt about Kelley's work, had his editors been vigilant and diligent. They were not."

- Staffers and government officials had been complaining about Kelley's work for years and never acted until— ironically—they got an anonymous complaint shortly after the *New York Times*/Jayson Blair debacle went down.

Here is the saddest irony of all. Kelley's editors repeatedly allowed him to use "anonymous sources." In other words, he didn't need to tell his editors exactly who was giving him information or why he believed they were competent to give it. *USA Today's* rulebook gave Kelley carte blanche to make up his shadowy "sources." (Sound familiar? That's right, we'll be talking about the out-of-control use of anonymous sources when we convene the Trial of Dan Rather.) But here's the twist that's absolutely mind-boggling: In the *USA Today* investigators report, they state that the paper's "executive editor has told us that he thinks these rules are as good as those in place at the *Washington Post*."

The *Washington Post*?

Can you believe it? The paper whose "rules" produced Janet Cooke and a scandal that's often billed as "the worst journalistic fraud of all time." The reaction of the *USA Today* investigators to the executive editor's plaintive "must-be-okay-if-the-*Post*-does-it" rationalization elicited this hilariously stiff reaction: Such rules "are not good enough for *USA Today*." The group slammed editing standards on the use of unnamed sources as "appallingly lax"—including one rule "which does not require that the reporter divulge the source to an editor in every instance."

Unbelievable!

For my *Enquirer* column, I produce—with the help of a hard-charging staff—an average of seventeen stories. A copy is immediately moved to our research department, which checks every checkable fact. Before I publish, the editor and/or the executive editor and our lawyers peruse with agonizing thoroughness an exhaustive list of every last source. Sources are not only named; there is an explanation for how each source cited could reasonably know the information attributed to them. It's a process that drives me up the wall, of course. After all, I'm the reporter/editor of three major pages, highly trusted, excruciatingly careful, with a reputation for accuracy over many years.

On my paper, I'm sort of a Jack Kelley—only in the sense, may I hasten to add, that I'm on a first-name basis with all our big shots. And, like Jack, I preen like a diva and talk about my news adventures on TV, on radio, at lectures and journalism schools—Columbia School of Journalism and the prestigious Berkeley included—and . . . and so what? None of it matters when it comes to delivering the goods. That's why my copy is checked and edited as rigorously as that of the *Enquirer* reporter who just walked in the newsroom door. No one in our business should be a law unto himself—not Mike Walker, not Jack Kelley, and not Dan Rather.

Journalists routinely gnash teeth and moan about editors tromping all over their precious copy, but good journalists welcome good editing, albeit grudgingly. Editing rescues you from dumb mistakes and foggy writing. A vigilant editing staff—management and operational—communicates and corrects, guides and challenges. It is the only effective sentinel against the evil that can creep on silent feet into the sound and fury of a newsroom, remaining undetected as it destroys from within.

The most infamous example of this system breaking down occurred at the *New York Times,* which concluded that the ongoing failure—finally detected in May 2003—"made it possible for a junior reporter . . . to get past one of the most able and sophisticated newspaper editing networks in the world."

As we all know, his name was Jayson Blair.

Chapter 8

Until this writing, I had never actually pored over the ninety-five-page report documenting the *New York Times* investigation into the notorious fabrication scandal that shamed the so-called "newspaper of record." It is a déjà vu eyeopener, a shocking reprise of the all-too-familiar newsroom ills documented by the *USA Today* investigation. And right at the top of the list, standing triumphant and glowering balefully, was our old nemesis—the demon that keeps cropping up in these horror tales of Media Elite screw-ups:

Fear!

In the *New York Times* investigation of the Blair Affair conducted by the usual suspects—a blue-ribbon panel of journalistic experts—the team backtracked, digging deep to unearth the well points of the quagmire, asking the staff and even the public for help in tracing their missteps. An outpouring of accusations were received and duly investigated. The final report stated:

Many of these complaints, both signed and anonymous, were from *Times* colleagues who said they had been afraid to speak out before—intimidated by the authoritarian style of top editors and by a culture that variously discouraged and neglected candid communications between people and departments working side by side. *Clearly the story of Jayson Blair was no longer just about him, perhaps not even principally about him.*

The italics are mine. To get quickly to the point—which is well-documented in the report—Jayson Blair managed to ruin the reputation of the *New York Times* mostly because a snotty, mean-tempered SOB named Howell Raines had been terrorizing the *Times* newsroom since taking over as executive editor in 2001. Blair, a personable, smooth talker *a la* his *USA Today* con-man counterpart Jack Kelley, had ingratiated himself to some degree with Raines, then started bragging around the newsroom about his friendly "relationship" with the much-feared executive editor and another major player, Managing Editor Gerald Boyd. As the report puts it, there was "a whiff of favoritism in the newsroom, a sense—advanced by Blair himself—that he had friends in high places at the paper . . . [and there was] a perception that some reporters had come to be favored in a 'star system' by the executive editor, Howell Raines, and from the fact that, like Blair, Gerald Boyd, who was then managing editor, is black."

Once again, the stage was set for mischief.

Jayson Blair's tale is high drama worth the telling, and—as I near the end of this book on a tight deadline—*Vanity Fair* magazine's December 2004 edition lands on my desk with an excerpt from a new book about the Blair case written by Seth Mnookin. It's called *Hard News: The Scandals at the New York Times and Their Meaning for American Media*. Apparently, the author is bent on kicking some media ass using the Blair

Affair as a catalyst, just as I'm hanging this book on Dan Rather—or am I hanging Dan Rather with this book? At any rate, I welcome Mnookin to the killing ground with open arms. His book arrives in timely fashion, just as some skeptical readers of this treatise might be saying restlessly to themselves, "Look, Walker, you've been hard-selling your B-movie headline—'Fear Stalks Our Newsrooms'—but is it possible that your premise is symptomatic of your own near-legendary paranoia? Are your tabloid roots showing in your near-obsessive compulsion to root endlessly for lurid plots like a hog for truffles?"

Well, pish and posh, you doubters! My answer to the first question is: All journalists—the good ones, anyway—are paranoid. My answer to the second: *Oink!*

So now comes the fresh voice of Mnookin, he of the Middle Earthish name, who writes the following hard-hitting—one might even say, lurid—words about the evil miasma of fear that permeated the *New York Times* newsroom, and the effect fear imposes on a newsgathering operation:

"There was such fear of [Howell] Raines's temper and dismissive attitude that some editors said they kept to themselves concerns about shoddy stories or reporters. A newsroom where editors are scared to voice their concerns is a disaster waiting to happen. Even worse is the newsroom where concerns were raised but ignored by the top editors."

So, I am a lone voice crying in the wilderness no longer. More and more concerned voices are being raised in the wake of epidemic shoddiness in the journalism practiced by the so-called Media Elite. Not loudly enough, perhaps, but, are you *listening*, News Snobs? Awake and mend your myopic ways before it's too late. Public trust in the Fourth Estate fades apace. Mobs of angry peasants swarm at the gates, brandishing pitchforks and torches!

Getting back to young Mr. Blair: the tragedy that's never been discussed at any length is the awful reality that this lying, arrogant ingrate not only blew an opportunity that was literally a dream come true for any aspiring journalist, he did it at the expense of some other talented minority youngster who should have been chosen in his place. Jayson Blair got a shot at stardom to die for. I would have died for it when I was a kid, fantasizing about becoming a newspaperman for the *New York Times,* or the *New York Daily News,* or my hometown *Boston Globe.* In my mind's eye, I was Frankie Flynn, Ace Reporter—one of those pushy guys in cheap suits you'd see in film *noir,* milling around in police stations yelling stuff like, "Come on, lieutenant, I'm on deadline—you got a suspect yet?" One can only imagine the thrill of being told: You've been chosen to intern at the Times. Stupidly, pathological liar Jayson Blair not only blew the chance of a lifetime, he savaged the reputation of his benefactors—then had the gall to hint darkly of reverse racism in the title of his dreadful failure of a book, *Burning Down My Master's House.*

What's most fascinating about the *Times* investigation is the observation mentioned above, that the story of Jayson Blair was "no longer just about him." He did not concoct and get away with his schemes in a vacuum. Incredibly, the report concludes that while there's no question the old Gray Lady got taken for a wild ride by a wet-behind-the-ears hustler, the embarrassing fact is that a classy dame who should have known better giddily hiked her skirts and kicked up her heels just too damn easily. This is why her chagrined morning-after mea culpa stunned the world when it ran on page one of the *New York Times,* May 11 2003:

> A staff reporter for the New York Times committed frequent acts of journalistic fraud while covering significant new events in recent months, an investigation by *Times* Journalists has found. The widespread fabrication and plagiarism represent a profound betrayal of trust and a low point in the 152-year history of the newspaper. The reporter, Jayson Blair, misled readers and Times colleagues with dispatches that purported to be from Maryland, Texas and other states, when often he was far away, in New York. He fabricated comments. He concocted scenes. He lifted material from other newspapers and wire services. He selected details from photographs to create the impression he had been somewhere, or seen someone, when he had not.

Bad enough. But then came the truly wicked details so reminiscent of the emotional ruthlessness displayed by *USA Today's* Jack Kelley. Jayson Blair, said the *Times,* "used these techniques to write falsely about emotionally charged moments in recent history, from the deadly sniper attacks in suburban Washington to the anguish of families grieving for loved ones killed in Iraq."

Jayson Blair, an African-American college student who

worked on the University of Maryland newspaper, came to the *Times* in an intern program "intended to increase newsroom diversity." The *Times* hired him based on good reviews from the university faculty. But after he was unmasked as a fraud, some thirty former student newspaper colleagues wrote that his disgraceful behavior "resembled a recurring pattern we witnessed." Ironically, they had tried to warn the faculty, but got nowhere. In four years at the *Times,* Blair wrote some six hundred stories—many of them totally phony—and eventually rose to the status of reporter on the national desk. If you wrote his saga as fiction, it would be deemed unbelievable.

Blair kept hopping nimbly from success to even loftier success, a mountain goat that never slipped. And it all worked so wonderfully because he'd devised a secret technique that was tailor-made for the *Times*—probably, in part, because no one had ever tried it before—but certainly because, in the words of the report, "a failure to communicate—to tell other editors what some people in the newsroom knew—emerges as the single most consistent cause . . . of this catastrophe. In the *New York Times* newsroom, silos had replaced sharing." Jayson Blair, genius *manqué* and outrageous charlatan, had hit upon a foolproof formula that fueled his amazing rocket ride from the interns' back bench to the front page of the *Times*. Like most breakthrough ideas, his technique was astoundingly simple at its core: *Better lies, better assignments.*

Jayson Blair lived by that mantra and led a charmed life. In the supposedly skeptical milieu of the newsroom, he discovered that no lie was too far-fetched. He was unstoppable, even when, in February 2002, Metro Editor Jonathan Landman attempted to shoot down Blair with an extremely negative evaluation. Landman forwarded his assessment to Managing Editor Gerald Boyd and to Associate Managing Editor Bill Schmidt, who was in charge of newsroom administration. The cover note read: "There's big trouble I want you both to be aware of."

And if that warning wasn't enough to command their attention, Landman led off his memo with a bombshell that should have blown Blair's cover once and for all. Wrote Landman: "We have to stop Jayson from writing for the *New York Times*. Right now."

Unbelievably, Jayson Blair was not frog-marched immediately out of the newsroom and told that his personal belongings would be sent to him after his desk was searched. Apparently, the *New York Times* is far too benevolent for that sort of crude behavior. As one manager later put it to the investigators of the sordid Blair Affair: "This is a compassionate organization. . . . We don't know how to fire people."

Fire the liar? Oh, heavens! That's the sort of thing they'd do on that wicked *National Enquirer,* darlings. No, let's keep poor Jayson on staff. Let's . . . well, let's pray for him. Or send him on leave for a while to straighten out his . . . er, problems . . . one of which, apparently, is something about drugs. Let's not be hasty.

But, wait. Why aren't we thinking of the reader? Won't the reader suffer if we keep a pathological liar on the staff?

Oh, tut tut, worrywarts. Let's just keep giving Jayson . . . bigger assignments! Let's send him off to cover a major story that's gripped the entire nation—how about that sniper thing?

Unbelievably, despite Landman's memo, that's just what the *New York Times* did. Here is what the investigators had to say, in hindsight, about that bizarre decision: "Much has been made of the fact that Blair's Oct. 30 story, 'U.S. Sniper Case Seen as a Barrier to a Confession,' got into the paper with five unidentified sources. . . . Given his problems with accuracy and what we now know to be his fabrication, the idea that he would have been given that level of trust on a complicated page 1 story is breathtaking."

Breathtaking!

That is the perfect, purple-prose word. The most dramatic tabloid writer—myself included—couldn't punch up that headline. It is truly the most appropriate way to describe the total breakdown of responsible editing that uncannily mirrors the earlier debacles of Janet Cooke/*Washington Post* and Jack Kelley/*USA Today*.

And, dear reader, I'm sure your keen eye blinked when you spotted that other pithy phrase you've come to know so well in your perusal of this diatribe about the Media Elite gone mad—the reference to "five unidentified sources" used to back up a page-one story. Sound familiar? Remember Janet Cooke being allowed to use unnamed sources? And you'll recall Jack Kelley getting a permanent exemption from identifying his "sources" on the most sensational page-one stories, year after year after year? What the *Times* investigation discovered was, in the words of Yogi Berra, déjà vu all over again. The report states:

It is notable that in our inquiry into the Blair scandal, several key editors gave differing answers on the number of corroborating sources we demand when granting anonymity, and on who at the paper must know their identity. *All of these editors assumed there was a paperwide policy on such matters. In fact, there has been none.*

Ka-pow! The smoking gun!

Again, those italics are mine—to emphasize that mind-boggling admission. Before this, I never would have believed anyone who tried to tell me that no firm editorial standards for identifying sources were in place at the *New York Times*. But there we see it, stark and dark on the page for all eternity—an infamy belatedly recorded by "the paper of record." Breathtaking, indeed!

In the *Times* report, investigators speak of "Choke Points"—their label for crucial moments when alarm bells should have jangled warnings about Jayson Blair. Choke Point 1 was missed when the *Times* failed to check his Maryland University background carefully. The *Times* actually had two bites at the apple on this because after a period of internship, Blair asked for time off to finish earning his bachelor's degree. When he returned to the *Times*, it was simply assumed he'd earned his degree. He had not—and nobody checked his story. That was Choke Point 2. "The paper now employs an outside firm to verify backgrounds," says the report.

Choke Point 3 came in late 2000. Blair was promoted to the regular full-time staff of the *New York Times*, despite committing "more mistakes than anyone else on metro; seven in just over two months" earlier that year. Said the report: "This step has all the earmarks of a social promotion. The recommendation was made by a recruiting committee led by Gerald Boyd. . . ."

Talk about friends in high places. No wonder Jayson Blair was able to intimidate lower-ranking editors into believing the fix was in for his starry rise. Said Metro Editor Landman: "The racial dimension of this issue and Gerald's obvious strong feelings made it especially sensitive; in that sense it is fair to say that I backed more than I would have if race had not been a factor. I think race was the decisive factor in his promotion." Landman goes on to say that he believes firmly in diversity for the *Times,* but "I emphatically do not believe that it is necessary to promote weak or troubled people in the name of diversity."

Now that he had the gig, Blair went sideways. He came in late, missed meetings, took long smoke breaks, and was defiant to his immediate supervisor, editor Jeanne Pinder, who kept trying to straighten out his sorry ass. His staggering arrogance resonates in a memo he sent her. It ended, "I am on your team—insomuch as it does not run afoul of what I need to do for myself."

A snotty crack like that—in writing—would have been a career-ender in the *Enquirer* newsroom. Arrogance aside, it shows pathetic judgment. But Jeanne Pinder had nowhere to go for help in controlling her nose-thumbing rogue. Jayson had juice.

One of his truly creepy lies—which should have raised suspicions but didn't—came in the wake of the 9/11 terrorist attack. Assistant Managing Editor Bill Schmidt compiled a list of *Times* family casualties, and Blair submitted the name of a "cousin" who'd died in the attacks. Later, he called Schmidt and withdrew the name before it made the final list. The subsequent investigation, of course, discovered that Blair had lost no one in 9/11.

Even Blair's big-shot buddy, Gerald Boyd, finally sensed something was seriously amiss and called him on the carpet. "I don't know what you're doing, drugs or what, and I don't care," Boyd told him, according to the report, "Unless you change, you are blowing a big opportunity."

Drugs?

In the words of the *Times* editor quoted earlier, "This is a compassionate organization." Turning a blind eye to possible drug addiction affecting a reporter's work is not compassion. It's dereliction of duty. How about a *Times* editor showing some compassion for folks who plunk down a buck a day for your paper, pal? And *five* bucks on Sunday. Learn the lesson I keep drumming into your lizard brains, Media Elite! You will *never* go wrong if you . . . (all together now, class) *always think of the reader!*

Immediately ferret out your liars, your junkies, your liar-junkies—and fire them all. Right *now!* Your readers deserve reliable news, not pot/crack/coke/smack-induced fantasies. The *Times* had that opportunity, but chose "compassion." So Jayson Blair slipped like a greased pig past Choke Point 4.

By now, you're probably wondering: What the hell ever happened to that "Jayson must stop writing for the *Times*" memo Landman sent Boyd? Well . . . nothing really. Howell

Raines, eternally busy spreading fear and loathing in the newsroom, told investigators he'd never laid eyes on it. "I regard it as highly unusual that I didn't get it," he said. For non-journalists who might wonder at this, you're absolutely right to question how this could be, so let me assure you that a newsroom operates, politically, like any other office. So can you imagine, at your workplace, Mr. Big-Big Shot not knowing that one of his junior Big Shots had written a memo condemning a staffer—you, for example—as too damn dangerous to be working there anymore? Enquiring minds might suspect that Howell Raines was . . . fibbing? If not, then the report is correct that the *Times* had devolved into a silo culture in which words like "office grapevine" and "water cooler gossip" had no meaning. The rule was: Nobody speaks to nobody . . . so to speak.

Long-suffering Jeanne Pinder—who was getting nowhere trying to tweak Blair's pals in high places—manfully came up with a written plan to manage her charge more strictly. Care to guess what Gerald Boyd said to that? Uh-huh, you got it. Gerald Boyd said unh-*unh!* Instead, with the approval of the higher-ups, Blair was suddenly moved to the sports desk. Boyd cited a "fresh start," and all the other baloney managers babble about when they can't solve a problem. Jeanne Pinder warned the sports editor in an e-mail: "If you see any slippage, or any signals of the sort of difficulties that have tripped him up in the past, you need to let me know." But the sports editor never called.

Yea, Jayson! Just passed Choke Point 5, dogg!

Blair worked just two weeks in sports, but still managed to

leave his slimy tracks. He phonied a story about Kent State that quoted the school's associate athletic director. Problem: The guy denied ever meeting Blair. And Blair had lifted, without attribution, story material from the *San Jose Mercury News*. Kent State later told investigators they'd kept trying to reach the *Times,* but guess what? Nobody home—sorreee! The sports editor recalled that he was "away" during that period. Oh.

The Blair Express picked up speed, whipping right through Choke Point 6. In an astoundingly stupid move, he suddenly was shifted to the prestigious national desk. The *Times* was getting beaten on the Washington-area sniper story by the *Baltimore Sun* and the *Washington Post* and wanted to beef up its reporting team. And who suggested Jayson? *Surprise!* "[Gerald] Boyd thinks it was he who brought up Blair's name," says the report. "There is no evidence that Blair's immediate supervisors were consulted."

Woooo-wooooo! Train's past Choke Station now! Four years of "extraordinary inaccuracies, disciplinary issues, unexplained absences, 'personal problems' " were ignored by Boyd & Company. Worse, none of them told any of it to Blair's new boss, National Editor Jim Roberts. The report states: "Not one of these managers can be found to have uttered any word of warning to National until Blair's sniper work came under challenge."

"This was an invitation to disaster. The invitation was accepted."

Gets harder to believe, doesn't it? Moans the *Times report:* "Attentive management would have required a history check.

Minimally collegial management would have dictated conversation among several people who knew, conversation that would at least have put Blair's national work under greater scrutiny, if it did not scuttle the assignment entirely."

The silo atmosphere in the newsroom evolved out of fear instigated by Executive Editor Howell Raines. In the aftermath of the Blair Affair, he was suddenly experiencing the fear of losing his job. He reacted like a scorpion poked with a stick. In his new book, Mnookin interviewed the journalists who conducted the internal investigation and were subjected to the autocratic executive editor's furious resentment at being forced to finally endure relentless and much-deserved scrutiny. He couldn't seem to grasp that his arrogant disregard for the professionals he was supposed to lead and inspire had led to the tragic breakdown in communication that besmirched 152 years of journalistic pride.

Says Mnookin, "Yes, Blair was a sociopath. But there had been ample warnings, and at times Raines and Boyd seemed to have pointedly ignored those warning because of their disdain for the editors who were doing the warning."

Boyd, who was widely perceived as turning a blind eye to Blair's glaring problems because he is African-American, took a different tack: deny, deny, deny. In the report, his disingenuous attitude induces nausea. "Philosophically, I have never bought into the concept of monitoring," he told investigators with a straight face. "I didn't feel I should take people under my wing and move them up the ladder. I incurred some criticism from journalists of color who felt I was not looking out for them."

Uh, huh. Not from Jayson Blair, I'll bet!

Proving that they're not suffering from total irony deficiency, the *Times* report then delivers my favorite line: "The rest is, unhappily, history."

The scourge was loosed. Remember Blair's story with "five unidentified sources"? It claimed that the White House had ordered federal prosecutors to interrupt the interrogation of the sniper suspect John Muhammad. Immediately, there was a federal denial. The Times later corrected Blair's story. Next, Robert Horan, the commonwealth attorney in Fairfax County, Virginia, actually called a press conference to denounce another Blair story about the sniper case. "The *Times* corrected two errors of fact," said the report, "that the evidence included a videotape from the Home Depot parking lot in Falls Church, Virginia, and that it included a grape stem with suspect Lee Malvo's saliva on it."

Gerald Boyd got very nervous about Horan's complaint, and finally brought National Editor Roberts up to speed on Blair's wonky history. Incredibly, even this revelation was not enough to bring down Jayson Blair. In the report, Roberts claims he just sort of . . . forgot about it. "It got socked in the back of my head," he recalls. Guess what happened then?

Jayson got a pay raise! In yet another left-hand-don't-know-what-the-right-hand's-doing cluster-bleep, an editor assigned to check pay lists found that Blair was lower paid than other reporters in his grade. Not knowing his history, he authorized the salary hike.

By this time, March 2003, the sniper case had died down a bit, so Blair was assigned to write home-front stories about the war in Iraq. He did a raft of stories about the family of Jessica Lynch. He pretended to be in West Virginia when he was in New York. He'd work with editors via e-mail and cell phone, leading them to believe he was on the scene when he was actually on another floor of the *Times* building or at home in Brooklyn. He concocted his stories by stealing quotes from wire service stories and making up details. He invented a dream that Jessica's mother supposedly had—then stupidly misspelled her name. He claimed to have spoken to a relative of Jessica's, who doesn't recall meeting him, and he conjured up a touching description of nonexistent "tobacco fields and cattle pastures" supposedly visible from the Lynch home.

The monstrous deception went on and on—until Blair filed a story about a Texas woman whose son was the only American soldier still missing in action in Iraq. It was a dead steal from a story in the *San Antonio Express-News*. Ironically, it was written by a reporter who had once been an intern at the *Times* and knew Blair. She phoned a Times contact, who told Gerald Boyd. He went to Jim Roberts, and finally, the liar was caught red-handed. He was summoned to the *Times* on April 29. Rather than produce expense reports that would prove he'd been in Texas, Jayson Blair resigned. A few weeks later, Gerald Boyd and Howell Raines were fired.

Here's the upbeat ending for the *New York Times:* Unlike CBS and Dan Rather, they knew that a cover-up is always worse than the crime. They immediately launched a thorough, no-holds-barred investigation, went public with it in less than two weeks, axed guilty parties, and began plugging the holes in their system. Their confession was swift and unflinching—unlike the agonized, grudging apology that the press and "pajama-clad bloggers" finally forced from Dan Rather and CBS.

From the evidence to date, it appears that the *New York Times* will be wary of allowing fear to fester in their newsroom. So, is true reform underway? It is—but it won't succeed if they revert to their hoity-toity ways and presume that everything's fine because they're the *Times*. It's a venerable organization with a long, proud history. Let's hope they do not succumb once more to that Media Elite affliction that inspired this treatise. You'll remember the word:

Hubris.

Speaking of which, it's time to convene the Court and conduct the Trial of Dan Rather.

Chapter 9

Hear ye, hear ye! Draw near for the Trial of Dan Rather! Hewing to the time-honored tradition of frontier justice as practiced in his home state of Texas, we will give Dan Rather a fair trial—then hang the sorry SOB!

Ironically, Rather's sudden retirement as anchorman of CBS News hits the headlines as we near the end of our treatise—and just as we commence this trial. Let the record show that his actions, now and in the future, will make no difference to these independent proceedings. The same goes for the final report of the panel investigating the embarrassing debacle of Rathergate, whatever it may disclose. This Court stands by the authority vested in me as a journalist who—by inclination and training—can't resist rattling cages for fun, profit, and the occasional public benefit.

Let the record now reflect that Dan Rather, in the immortal words of Jack Nicholson, can't handle the truth! Not about himself, anyway, if we read this sudden, surprising retirement correctly. Truth—or spin? Here are the facts . . . you decide!

"Nobody's pushing me out," Rather told the *New York Daily News*. "I wouldn't steer you otherwise."

If you believe that, you'll believe rocks can grow, as Dan himself might say.

Few people recall it, but a mere two weeks after the Rathergate fiasco exploded across front pages, the embattled anchorman defiantly insisted—in response to questioning at a journalism seminar in New York—that he definitely was not planning to retire. Here's the quote, as emphasized in Chapter 1 of this book:

> I don't have a date [to retire]. . . . I don't have a timetable. I have a passion for what I do. I love what I do. As long as I like doing it, as long as I think I can do it at least reasonably well—and most importantly, as long as the people I work for think I can do it reasonably well, then I want to continue doing it.

Very clearly stated. But that was then—and this is now, apparently. Despite the unequivocal statement that he wouldn't retire under fire, Dan has rather suddenly changed his story, telling the *Daily News* he's been mulling retirement since the 9/11 attacks. In yet another interview, he went even further and suddenly shared the . . . er, "late-breaking" revelation that in summer of 2004—way back before the scandal broke—he and the CBS brass made the decision that he'd leave in 2005. Funny that he forgot to tell us that before.

And here's a bulletin for you suspicious folks with enquiring minds: Both Rather and CBS New President Andrew Heyward want to make one thing perfectly clear: the anchorman is *not* trying to short-circuit the investigation by getting out before a negative report recommends that he be thrown out. Perish the thought!

"The fact is, we've been talking about this for a long time," insisted Heyward.

Uh-huh. Sure you have.

Little wonder the *New York Post* ran a savage cartoon showing candidates for Dan's anchor chair lining up at CBS for job interviews. Prospects include Pinocchio, Baghdad Bob, Jayson Blair, the Boy Who Cried Wolf, and a Liar-Liar-Pants-on-Fire guy. Another chuckle-evoker in a relentless series of Rather-biased cartoons was one depicting Dan and Janet Jackson with the caption, "CBS Exposed Boobs!"

So, did Dan jump? Or was he shoved?

Shortly after the Rathergate scandal, the *New York Times* quoted a longtime colleague of the CBS News star, who said that March 2006 was a date of great significance to Rather. That's when he'd celebrate his twenty-fifth anniversary as anchorman of the evening news. The colleague said that the date had become even more important to Rather after the scandal.

"If I'm him, I want to hang on so I can try to put it back together," the colleague said. "He is so, by nature, a fighter. He's a dog with a bone. I just don't see him letting go. He's too proud of what he's accomplished as a journalist."

Let the record reflect that the Court finds the following testimony from an expert witness powerful and persuasive. Marvin Kalb, Rather's colleague of twenty-five years at CBS News, stated flatly that the investigative panel's report "is undoubtedly going to be negative, and what CBS is doing now is removing Dan Rather from the line of fire," according to the *Los Angeles Times*.

Media experts scoffed at Rather's contention that it's his unforced decision to retire from his anchor post, pointing out that under normal circumstances, neither he nor CBS would make the public relations gaffe of announcing it just one week before Tom Brokaw's highly ballyhooed retirement. It's obvious CBS and Rather rushed to get under the wire with the announcement because they're expecting the long-over-due findings of the investigators—and indeed, anticipate that they'll be negative.

The Court hereby decrees that we do not need to hear more on this point. Let the record reflect our belief that Rathergate has forced Dan Rather's exit from the anchor booth. He does not go gently into that good night.

Note: The Court will make peremptory judgments as we proceed because we cannot, as a practical matter, consult with you, the jury. This is only a book and, sadly, not interactive. Judge Walker is, therefore, The Man. Order in de court, 'cause here come de judge!

Now, let's get down to the real business before the Court, to wit: is Dan Rather guilty of journalistic high crimes and misdemeanors? What did he do, why did he do it, and does justice demand that he be fired from the network, or do we simply allow him to ease on down the road? Let's look at this bizarre case, step by step, from the moment in 2003 when Dan Rather says it all began. At that time, the CBS anchorman—like other diligent news diggers looking for major scoops relating to the Bush-Kerry contest—was hot on the trail of persistent allegations that George W. Bush had not fulfilled his service obligations in the National Guard. There were gaps in his official records that did not explain, for instance, why he had missed a required pilot's physical.

Rather and his CBS News producer Mary Mapes—who'd

won kudos for breaking the Abu Ghraib prison abuse scandal just months before—had heard whispers about documents that would fill in those blanks and embarrass the president. In Rather's words he and Mary Mapes were "working the story."

In early 2003, they made contact with a Texas farmer and former National Guard officer named Bill Burkett. He was making the astounding claim that years ago he'd overheard aides to then-Texas Governor George W. Bush ordering National Guard officials to delete anything potentially embarrassing in his service files. Even though Burkett had nothing to back up this shocking claim, he went public with it in February 2004. He appeared on such TV shows as MSNBC's *Hardball*, attracting attention from the White House—which denied his allegations—and from the so-far-elusive "mystery woman" Lucy Ramirez. In his ever-changing story of how he came by the phony documents, Burkett would claim that "Ramirez", a stranger, phoned to say she'd seen him on *Hardball* and had "something" relevant to his Bush jihad that needed to be revealed.

Despite the White House denials of Burkett's allegations, Mapes continued to cultivate the former Guard officer, believing—or wanting to believe—that he was the key to finding "smoking gun" documentation that would back up his tale.

Did Mapes—an experienced TV producer—check out her source, Bill Burkett, thoroughly? Rudimentary research would have revealed him to be the type of personality good journalists recognize quickly and are wary of—the ding-dong with an ax to grind. Burkett was well documented, if you will, as a disgruntled retiree from the National Guard, who claims he was unfairly denied medical treatment for a service-related disorder. He has a lurid history as a vocal George Bush hater. He has denounced his fellow Texan as a "Hitler" and "Napoleon." Burkett also suffers from self-admitted mental problems.

Did Mapes acquaint herself with Burkett's bizarre record? If so, how to justify placing such complete faith in an obviously flawed source? Remember, Mapes vouched for Burkett to her boss, Rather, who ended up looking like a fool when he insisted that his source was "unimpeachable." It's important to emphasize, however, that he was the boss. Mapes couldn't force him into anything. Unless the record shows that she kicked and screamed in protest—a highly unlikely scenario—Mapes was either caught up in her own jihad or incompetent. Or a bit of both. In the Court's experience, TV producers are often not very well trained as journalists. "Image" is paramount in their approach to news. To get the right image, they'll manipulate and bend facts without much soul-searching.

Here's an example of what I'm talking about, as exposed in my *National Enquirer* column back in 1994, just after I wrote *Nicole Brown Simpson: Private Diary of a Life Interrupted,* my *New York Times* Number One bestseller on the O. J. Simpson case. The item ran as follows:

Hang down your head in shame, Diane Sawyer! On your September 15 *Prime Time Live* you duped viewers into thinking that they were looking at Nicole Simpson's grave when you showed her headstone. You EVEN grouped flowers around the marker to make it look like a real gravesite—thereby milking America's tears. But I'd already told my readers that the family has NEVER placed the headstone on her grave for fear of vandals and 'souvenir' hunters. After your show aired, we viewed the gravesite—and the headstone wasn't there. A family source confirmed your deception, saying producers simply photographed the headstone on a LAWN! (I phoned Diane for her side of the story, but she wouldn't respond.)

How's that for a sleazy move? Effective, of course, and nobody was harmed by it, but, you're either tabloid or you're not, Media Elite! And to think that you guys have the nerve to sneer at the *National Enquirer.* Come to think of it, Diane's producer was trained at the *National Enquirer* by—among other editors—Mike Walker. So I've only myself to blame.

Again, the motivation of TV journalists differs from print journalists. They are in the business of producing moving pictures. They need people and scenes and objects that can be photographed—documents, for instance. Mapes desperately wanted documents she believed existed that would discredit George Bush. Her boss, Dan Rather, needed something tangible to wave around on TV. Mapes prayed Burkett would deliver the goods. He didn't.

Interestingly, the *Wall Street Journal,* in an editorial page piece by Holman W. Jenkins, wrote:

The enduring mystery remains. Whom does CBS hire as its "news producer"? . . . [A]nybody who looks at archival documents with any frequency is smacked in the eyes by the difference between typewritten and computer-generated products. The real problem here, though, is the hunt by TV news producers of mediocre intelligence for 'scoops'—which increasingly means artificial attempts to infuse information with drama suitable to an entertainment program.

CBS News producer Mary Mapes kept after Burkett, and she kept digging in the Lone Star State. In August 2003, she phoned a Texas man named Gary Killian. His father had been Bush's commanding officer in the National Guard. She asked for his help in locating documents criticizing Bush that had allegedly been written by his father. Killian was unhelpful. He told Mapes that he and his stepmother seriously doubted that any such documents had ever been written because his father had thought well of George Bush.

Mapes was stymied. She made contact again with Burkett. He met her and CBS reporter Mike Smith at a pizza eaterie near his Texas ranch. He handed the surprised reporters two of six documents. Suddenly, Mapes was back in business. Then, on the Friday before Labor Day—a miracle! She phoned Rather with great news: Bill Burkett had agreed to turn over four more documents and complete the set. Rather immediately jetted to Texas to get his oh-so-necessary moving pictures—an interview with Burkett buttressed by the visual of documents that were sheer dynamite. If authentic, they could potentially bring down a sitting president of the United States. There was no time to waste. Other journalists were working the Texas National Guard angle. The Bush-Kerry race was neck-and-neck—and Election 2004 was less than two months away.

It was a supercharged moment. Dan Rather's heart caught

fire as he laid eyes at last on Bill Burkett's bombshell memos, allegedly from the files of Lt. Col. Jerry B. Killian, George W. Bush's long-deceased commanding officer in the Texas Air National Guard. There it was in an official memo: the sensational claim that Killian had been pressured by big shots to "sugar coat" Bush's record as a flying officer.

Wow!

Then, a major glitch! The smoking gun wasn't quite ready to fire. Burkett refused to tell Rather how the damning documents had come into his hands. Incredibly, the anchorman would later insist that he and Mapes had hammered Burkett to identify the source of the documents, saying, "We made it very clear that the chain of possession was very important to us." Really? The Court finds that hard to believe, Mr. Rather! Aren't you the much-advertised reporter who asks tough questions and demands the right answers?

The Court directs your attention to the real "smoking gun" that triggered Rathergate: Even when Burkett finally "revealed" that the documents had been given to him by a former Texas National Guard officer now working in Europe for the U.S. Army, a George Conn, CBS News failed to contact Conn and verify that Burkett was telling the truth.

Stop! Don't go back and read it. Your eyes aren't lying. Dan Rather, hard-charging reporter, did *not* track down and question the primary source of serious charges against the president.

With respect, one reporter to another . . . how do you sleep at night?

Rather would later claim that his crack news team did verify George Conn actually existed, and that as a Guard officer he could possibly have had access to Killian's files. Yet somehow, ignoring the high standards he claims to hold, Rather didn't go face-to-face with George Conn. He didn't even give him a jingle. In one of the most staggering admissions this Court has ever heard from a journalist, Rather says he decided that once they'd established that George Conn actually existed, that alone was enough to justify using the story.

In his own words, "That made it believable."

In the Court's words: What's the frequency, Kenneth?

Is the needle pointing at crazy or dumb? Let the record show that this Court is bloody well gobsmacked that a $10-million-a-year anchorman—who proudly referred to himself as a "hard news investigative reporter" on the occasion of his recent . . . ahem . . . retirement could be such a naive *twit!* With respect, answer the question, sir. Was it naiveté? Or was it that Dan Rather just got sloppy because anti-Bush blood lust had him snortin' like a stallion in springtime? It's one or, *ipso facto*, it's the other.

In this Court's discovery phase, strict rules for dealing with "unidentified sources" were explained painstakingly. The Court demonstrated the horrors that ensued when the *Washington Post, New York Times, USA Today,* and others ignored this bedrock basis of journalism. That's how they were victimized by willful liars Cooke, Blair, and Kelley. In this case, the CBS reporters were not liars willfully concocting a phony story—but they certainly let one happen. Why? What rule should they have remembered? All together now . . .

Never fall in love with a story!

That's right. And CBS News/Rathergate is a perfect illustration. Here's another favorite homily I preach to reporters that also fits this situation:

Paper trails keep you out of jail!

If Mapes/Rather had confronted Conn and he'd supported Burkett's lie that he was the source of the documents, well . . . CBS still would have a wrong story. It's sad, but it happens. Sources sometimes lie. But then, CBS News staffers could say, hand on heart, that they'd done their best. Even if they'd tried to find Conn and failed, they'd be able to produce a "paper trail"—phone records, copies of e-mail and fax queries, etc.— that would prove they'd been professional, made best efforts, and simply been screwed over by liars. It's still not a happy result, but it wouldn't be Rathergate!

Working journalists everywhere are boggled that, for whatever reason, Mapes/Rather & Company were able to live with not nailing down an identifiable source. How? I'd be a nervous wreck. It had to bother them to some degree. Assuming it did (and it's hard to believe *somebody* didn't have a twinge of conscience), why didn't red flags pop up in Camp CBS when it was discovered that Burkett's damning documents were not only of mysterious origin, but worse, they were copies?

Copies, ladies and gentlemen.

Before dealing thoroughly with the issue of using copies to establish the authenticity of documents, here is the quick rule of thumb: *Fuhgeddaboudit!*

The Court will now make a sidebar relating to documents—including photos, artwork and the like—that come into the possession of news organizations. Common sense should tell anyone—much less "experienced journalists" such as Rather and Mapes—that trafficking in stolen items is illegal. The "chain of possession," as Rather correctly put it, is crucial. Whether you are the *New York Times,* CBS News, or the *National Enquirer,* you must be prepared to prove you are in legal possession of a document, photograph, map, etc., before you go to press with it.

The *National Enquirer* is a recognized pioneer in this area. What a proud breakthrough for journalism when the *Enquirer* pioneered the daring technique of pawing through the garbage of the rich and famous.

(SOUND OF GAVEL BANGING) Order! Order in the Court, right *now,* I say! Stifle those giggles, or I will clear this courtroom. We are engaged in serious business here. I will not tolerate indecorous outbursts of any kind.

That's better!

Now, by way of hypothetical example, it would be serious business indeed if investigative journalists somehow were *legally* allowed to search the desk or filing cabinets of high government officials suspected of hanky-panky. Who can forget the sensational worldwide headlines the *Enquirer* made when its reporters rummaged through Henry Kissinger's garbage— going where no newsmen had gone before—and discovered top-secret government documents that the careless Secretary of State Kissinger didn't shred before trashing, including his own Secret Service identity code. Garbage is a treasure trove. Archaeologists weep at its discovery as they excavate in the detritus of ancient civilizations. Garbage yields a road map to the soul; it's not just incriminating documents, but dirty pictures, drug paraphernalia, used-up sex toys, pregnancy kits, and—when Elizabeth Taylor's trash was cased—well-thumbed copies of the dreaded *National Enquirer.*

Point is, documents often materialize either in trash cans or en route to them. If that's where you found them, you're probably okay. That was established in law after the *Enquirer* started going right to the source, so to speak. Lawyers for the rich and famous fought to curtail our garbage-surfing, largely in vain—except for an ordinance that Beverly Hills town fathers passed at the behest of nervous celebs, which decreed that only municipal workers could haul trashcans away. But courts have upheld the right to garbage peek, ruling that once trash is deposited at the curb it is no longer yours. That's why it's important to prove where a document originated; hence, the chain of possession.

Ergo, document from garbage, probably okay—document stolen, not okay.

As for *copies* of documents, they're useless, except in a very limited way. First of all, you cannot determine from a copy if the original is authentic. With an original, a document expert can make tests to determine the type of ink and paper used; where information has been written over, typed over, or crossed out; whether signatures are genuine or have been altered, etc. To complicate matters further, today's digital technology and computers have made document forgery child's play. How easy to phony . . . a report card, for example. It's this simple: Electronically copy an authentic signature from a real document, tweak it in a Photoshop program, paste it into a bogus document and—voila!—you're a master forger. Your phony won't fool an expert, perhaps, but if the expert has only a copy of the document . . . well, you get the picture. Or rather, you won't get the picture.

Mary Mapes and Dan Rather contacted document analysis experts before running the Bush/National Guard "memos" on *60 Minutes*. In a *New York Times* article written post-Rathergate by Tom McNichol, document examiner Emily J. Will said she was asked to authenticate the documents from faxed photocopies. "Because the documents were copies, I couldn't see the fine details in the signature, like was a letter made clockwise or counterclockwise, or was the pen lifted," she said. "Without more information, like the original documents or more handwriting samples of the signature, there's no way you could have authenticated the documents."

No way!

The Court redirects your attention to that unequivocal judgment by Ms. Wills, an expert. Further, let the record show that Ms. Wills stated she specifically warned CBS it would face questions from document experts. The lady sure got that right! After the Rathergate storm broke, nearly every independent expert jeered at the documents and said they were produced by a modern word processor, not a typewriter circa the 1970s. The primary authenticator hired by CBS News, Marcel Matley, echoed Ms. Wills when he said there was "no way that I, as a document expert, can authenticate them." Even more embarrassing, there was no way Marcel Matley himself could be authenticated as a document expert. *Ow!*

Six days after CBS broadcast the Bush/National Guard story, the New York Post scooped that Matley—the man Rather called a "handwriting analyst and document expert who believes the material is authentic"—had admitted in a 1995 court deposition that he has no formal training as a document expert. A week later, NBC nailed the coffin closed with a report that identified Matley as a "former librarian whose only formal document training was a mail-in correspondence course."

CBS flack Sandy Genelius had a slick spin on the Matley revelation. "In the end, the gist is that it's inconclusive," she chirped.

You go, girl!

The Court has gotten a bit ahead of itself with what it considers necessary peroration on the use of documents in journalism, and will momentarily pick up the timeline of the Mapes-Rather adventures in gonzo journalism, but please indulge us in this bit of background first.

The Court stated earlier that "copies of documents are useless—except in a limited way." To illustrate, the *National Enquirer* also would have had the documents analyzed—using a standby cadre that includes FBI-trained experts—but would have nixed them as stand-alone proof after hearing they looked phonier than a Texas polar bear. If you hire experts, do not ignore their advice. *Enquirer* photo editors know from experience that today's digital technology means you sometimes need to authenticate photos. Experts crawled all over the *Enquirer's* headline-making photos of O. J. Simpson caught wearing the so-called "ugly-ass Bruno Magli shoes" he claimed he'd never owned—the ones that left his bloody footprint at that infamous crime scene. O. J. tried to brand them as fakes, but failed. Based on *Enquirer* photos endorsed by experts, the civil trial jury found him liable for double murder. Hooray for our team! Just imagine if those photos had surfaced during the criminal trial. O. J. would be roasting in hell this minute. (Just a matter of time, Juice!)

Ironically, Mapes and Rather still could have aired a provocative story, if only they'd admitted to themselves that the memos were only copies and possibly phony. Here's how: Put Burkett on the air, interviewing him as a former National Guard officer who's produced startling documents that he claims are real. You flash the memos onscreen. You explain to viewers that Burkett has revealed the name of the source that allegedly gave him the documents, and you've verified that his source is also a former Guard officer who could have known about Bush's service record. You tell viewers about Burkett's history as a malcontent Bush hater, and give him a chance to explain why that shouldn't disqualify him as a whistle-blower.

Next, you show clips of CBS correspondents in the field interviewing people connected to the Guard scene—saying they either believe or disbelieve Burkett. Now you've laid it all out frankly to your viewers. You add that CBS News experts cannot authenticate the memos because, sadly, they are copies, and Burkett does not have the original. You point out that the memos could be genuine and that Burkett was a Guard officer who could have overheard the "conversations" about whitewashing then-Governor Bush's records.

After presenting the whole story, you explain that you're

airing it because it's timely and provocative, especially considering charges and countercharges about the military records of Bush and Kerry that are inflaming passions in the election. Then—without endorsing the documents one way or the other—you speak to your viewers:

> RATHER: "Fact? Fiction? It's anybody's call. We got some
> answers, but clearly we need more. The question remains:
> why didn't George Bush take that pilot's physical?
> (INTO CAMERA, TALKING TO DUBYA)
> RATHER: With respect, sir—answer the question!"

It's a classic "You Decide!" story. The *Enquirer* does them; everybody does them. It's not quite as much fun as endorsing a wacko smear of the president—but it's an *accurate* story that's provocative enough to make headlines and get people talking around the water cooler.

If that sounds rather dumb, contrast it with your rush to judgment that suddenly accelerated like a runaway jet, despite (1) copies of documents your own experts wouldn't endorse heartily, from a biased source who (2) can't prove where the documents really came from, but (3) offered you a possible source that you never bothered to contact.

Dan Rather brags that he's not afraid to ask the tough questions. Is he afraid to do tough legwork? Or too lazy? He was just short of his seventy-third birthday but had a big team at his beck and call. Why didn't he track down George Conn? Rather claims loud and proud that he adheres to the highest journalistic standards. In one of seven books he's written about himself—with the aid of cowriters, of course; no keyboard calluses for this $10 million diva—Rather attributes his success to being damn careful and damn right! Of his early career and rocket ride to the top of the broadcast heap, he wrote:

"If I'd gone off half-cocked, if I'd gotten my facts scrambled, if I'd run with unconfirmed leads, I'd be selling insurance now."

Hello, Allstate?

So why—a scant three days after Mapes obtained the final documents from Burkett at the pizza joint—did Managing Editor/Anchorman Dan Rather rush the story on the air in the *60 Minutes* edition of September 8? Let's go through the timeline and reconstruct what happened.

After Mapes got the memos from Burkett, Rather took his hot Bush-bash story right to the top. In an interview on Monday, September 20, the day Rather and CBS finally admitted they'd blown it, the anchor told the *New York Times* that after learning Mapes had the documents in hand, he phoned Andrew Heyward, president of CBS News. In Rather's words: "This is not verbatim . . . but I said: 'Andrew, if true, it's breakthrough stuff. But I need to do something unusual. It may even be unique. I have to ask you to oversee, in a hands-on way, the handling of this story, because this is potentially the kind of thing that will cause great controversy.' He got it. He immediately agreed."

Cool. The Court applauds that cagey move, sir! As any veteran newsman knows, it's always a good move to drag a higher-up right into the mix—it cuts down on their deniability ("Who, me?"), making it somewhat tougher for them to throw you to the wolves if the story blows up. They'll still try, mind you . . . but it slows 'em up a bit. Thanks to Rather's foresight in getting his boss directly involved, Andrew Heyward became a person of great interest to the independent panel investigating the debacle.

After his conversation with Rather, according to the *New York Times*, Heyward immediately ordered a top deputy, Betsy West, to supervise the story's progress closely. And that's what, reportedly, she did. To quote an enquiring (and apparently suspicious) mind, *Los Angeles Times* media critic Tim Rutten noted: "With grease that thick on the rails, it's little wonder that less than a week passed between the time Mapes obtained the dubious memorandums from Burkett and Rather went on the air with the report."

Commenting on the unprecedented stonewalling and stumbling by Rather and CBS as their story crumbled, Rutten—a seasoned media observer—found it "difficult to recall a crisis-beset news organization of this caliber whose managerial and journalistic stewards have failed their audience and staff quite as thoroughly as CBS's have over the last two weeks."

In those final days and hours before airtime, the CBS team scrambled to make their shaky story stand up on its own two legs. The timeline—as a sequence of exactly what happened when—gets murky. At some point, experts hired to inspect the documents started warning of authentication problems. For some reason, they were ignored. Then the CBS lawyers screened the report and questioned producers about it—but not until the day of the broadcast.

Of all the moments in this truly historic newsgathering fiasco, this is the one that the Court cannot comprehend. Having endured this excruciating process literally thousands of times, it staggers the imagination to believe that attorneys experienced in vetting news reports let the story fly with no source for the documents, no chain of possession, no solid authentication by experts, Burkett's obvious bias, etc. Using the example of the *National Enquirer* again, the Court can state most assuredly that the paper's attorneys, faced with the same example, would take on that slightly constipated look lawyers get when clients blithely grease the rails for a rocket ride to court, and say to the editor: *Fuhgeddaboudit!*

My incredulity is shared by the *Wall Street Journal.* Two days after the CBS story broke—and the documents were instantly challenged by document experts and bloggers—it wrote this on its editorial page:

Perhaps *60 Minutes* reporters will finally learn the wisdom of consulting their company's own in-house lawyers, who've proved better, more skeptical journalists over the years than the journalists themselves. Here's a bet they would have taken one look at the purported Bush-incriminating National Guard documents and asked why they didn't look the way paperwork did in the early 1970s.

Intriguing. CBS claims their lawyers did vet the story, albeit at the last minute. Now the *Journal* questions whether that's actually true. Wouldn't that be a shocker? My guess: They did— but it's hard to believe they okayed it. The *Journal* points out in the same piece that the CBS legal eagles stopped the network "from going off the cliff in 1995 with a story about tobacco 'whistleblower' Jeffrey Wigand, who claimed he'd been subjected to a death threat for spilling the industry's beans. Never mind that an FBI investigator had already told the network that Mr. Wigand had faked the death threat himself. Mike Wallace and Co. ignored the evidence and prostrated themselves before a 'source' who was a liar and scam artist. . . ."

Hmm. A source with an ax to grind leads CBS reporters down the garden path. Sound familiar?

Like the *Wall Street Journal,* this Court knows how lawyers pounce on things like the credentials of so-called experts. It's so easy to be misled by charlatans. The *Journal* recalled in its piece that proud moment in tabloid history when the *Enquirer's* sister publication *Star* magazine broke the Gennifer Flowers-Bill Clinton sexy phone tapes. The CBS affiliate in Los Angeles sneered at the *Star,* then turned over the tapes to their "expert" for analysis—the so-called Hollywood private eye Anthony Pellicano. That gave all of us in the tabloid world— or should I call it the "real world"—a big laugh. We knew Pellicano, who is even now under investigation for illegal wiretapping. Working for CBS in L.A., Pellicano concluded that the tapes were "misleading" and "not credible." His "analysis" helped Big Horny Bubba survive the Flowers controversy, but CBS had been flim-flammed. The TV newsies were finally embarrassed when it came out that Pellicano had no formal training in evaluating tapes, and worse, that Democratic sources were secretly paying him for his lies to quell Clinton "bimbo eruptions." Not that Pellicano is unfamiliar with electronics. The LAPD uncovered evidence that he'd wire-tapped the phone of a *Los Angeles Times* reporter who'd been victimized by mysterious threats. Pellicano went up for a two-and-a-half-year stretch at a federal pen for possession of firearms and explosives.

Oh, those CBS "experts!"

Now, here is where the Court will ask *National Enquirer* gossip editor Mike Walker to make an educated guess. As a wily operator experienced in rescuing stories about to go up in flames, what do you think happened next, sir?

> WALKER: If it please the Court, there'd be just one way to make this turkey fly past any attorneys I know. I'd contact President Bush's reps and run it by them for comment. If the subject of a story doesn't deny what you've got, or only denies part of it, or denies without offering solid checkable facts that prove you're wrong, you can probably run the story—as long as you include their response. And sometimes you get really lucky, your Honor, especially on my celebrity news beat, because many PR reps are dumber than ant-eaters. Even when you phone and say you're about to run a story charging that their movie-star client smuggles and enslaves illegal aliens as a profitable sideline, they often don't even bother to call you back! Which is a big help if they raise hell later and claim your story is wrong, because a legal complaint would probably get tossed out on the grounds that they never responded to good-faith efforts to set the record straight.

THE COURT: Is that what happened here?

WALKER: Yes. CBS News contacted the White House and sent over the documents. But I find their method a bit . . . strange, your Honor.

THE COURT: Enlighten us, please.

WALKER: Well, sir, news is a deadline business, but the *Enquirer* tries to give people reasonable time to respond.

THE COURT: And how much time did CBS give the president of the United States to respond to decades-old, alleged documents impugning his military service—records that, it's important to add, he could never, by their very nature, have seen before because they were supposedly "secret" documents. Did Dan Rather & Company give President Bush, say, at least twenty-four hours?

WALKER: No, sir. They gave him three hours.

Three hours!?

According to the *New York Times,* the program's executive producer said that White House failure to question the documents after three hours gave CBS the effective go-ahead it needed to air the broadcast. White House Chief of Communications Dan Bartlett scoffed at the explanation, saying the president and others on his staff had scant time to check the accuracy of the documents. Furthermore, Bartlett huffed, their response could in no way be confused with being an endorsement of them.

The Court is appalled. Allowing the president, or anyone

just three hours to respond to a charge of military malingering—based on a document of murky provenance—seems manic, to say the least. And in this case Rather & Company didn't even have the excuse that a rival news organization was close to breaking the story. One senses the desperation underlying this rather hasty three-day rush to judgment back around September 7–8. There's an adumbration that Mapes/Rather knew they were sucking wind. They declined to phone the alleged source, George Conn, but they did phone another of Bush's superior officers in the Guard, a General Bobby Hodges, and asked him to vouch for the memos. Once the story blew up, CBS would claim that Hodges had endorsed the memos as authentic. Hodges protested, saying he'd never actually seen the memos—and once he did, he questioned their authenticity.

When CBS spokeswoman Sandy Genelius heard that, she responded by implying that Hodges was lying. "We believed General Hodges the first time we spoke to him," she snipped.

Hodges added an interesting tidbit: The officer who supposedly had pressured him to "sugar coat" Bush's record, a Colonel Walter Staudt, had actually left the Guard by the date of the memo.

Going back in the timeline to the September 8 airdate, another stunner rears its ugly head. Josh Howard, executive producer of the Wednesday edition of *60 Minutes,* admitted to the *New York Times* that even then—just hours before the broadcast—he did not know the source of the documents. He made inquiries of Mapes, he recalls, and she was able to satisfy him that any questions concerning their authenticity had been answered.

It all sounds so excitingly last minute, doesn't it? The lawyers see the piece at the eleventh hour, the executive producer doesn't know who the source of the story is and finally has to ask questions—apparently because he hadn't been monitoring its progress as it moved through the editing process. Is a story that slimes the president scant weeks before national elections just *routine* for the Media Elite?

Ah, entropy. Thy name is CBS News. No wonder Edward R. Murrow's ghost haunts its halls at night—or so Dan Rather told the *Hollywood Reporter* in a just-surfaced interview that quotes him confessing to actual conversations with the spectral icon of CBS News past. Rather now denies the interview, but no matter. From what I know of Ed Murrow, he's probably stopped speaking to Dan.

Chapter 10

Hit rewind. Reel back in time to September 8, 2004.

At CBS headquarters, the Manhattan skyscraper ominously known as Black Rock, Executive Producer Josh Howard is just hours away from pulling the trigger on the Wednesday night edition of *60 Minutes*. He breathes a sigh of relief. He'd had questions on the Bush/National Guard story. Up until the very day of broadcast, he had not known what sources the news team had to back up the piece. But producer Mary Mapes—who'd broken the Abu Ghraib prison abuse exposé in May—finally satisfied him on all points. Good old Mapes. A solid CBS News star. Go to the bank on her stuff. Slam-dunk.

Josh Howard might not have felt so calm and confident had he known that as she worked the story, Mary Mapes—described by the Associated Press as "a dogged and talented journalist who made no secret of her liberal political beliefs"—had phoned presidential candidate John Kerry's top campaign adviser, Joe Lockhart, and told him to call Bill Burkett. Mapes had a scoop, and she wanted to share it with the Kerry campaign. She told Lockhart that the ex-Guard officer, now retired on his Texas farm, had unearthed eye-opening memos concerning George Bush's military service.

It stunk to high heaven. With that phone call, Mary Mapes

forfeited all claims to being a nonbiased journalist. Reporting news that might swing a presidential election is one thing. Extending a helping hand to the side you've openly rooted for goes beyond the pale. No matter how you spin it, Mapes called Lockhart knowing she might be handing John "Swift Boat" Kerry the ammo he needed to blow George Bush out of the water.

Here is what the Associated Press reported after speaking to Lockhart: "'[Mapes] basically said there's a guy who is being helpful on the story who wants to talk to you,' Lockhart said—adding that it was common knowledge that CBS was working on a story raising questions about Bush's Guard service. Mapes told Lockhart there were some records 'that might move the story forward. She didn't tell me what they said.'"

As a savvy, longtime TV producer, Mapes—the forty-eight-year-old mother of two, married to a journalist—had to know she was breaking the rules. As a CBS spokesman later admitted: "It is obviously against CBS News standards and those of every other reputable news organization to be associated with any political agenda."

Why did Mapes flout ethics and risk her job? Bill Burkett—the inflamed fanatic bent on destroying George Bush—later told *USA Today* that the agreed-upon price for handing the memos over was that she'd get Kerry's campaign to call him. CBS denied that assertion. But Lockhart has confirmed that Mapes gave him Burkett's phone number. Her reason for arranging their conversation was either because, as Burkett claims, it was the "price" she had to pay for his documents—

or because she's a liberal Kerry fan. Either—or both, perhaps. Mapes had set the game in motion. Presidential candidate John Kerry's campaign adviser telephoned bilious Burkett—the man who refers to George Bush as "Hitler"—and the two total strangers had a conversation. Suppress the urge to holler "Liar, liar, pants on fire" when you hear Lockhart's version of what he and Burkett discussed.

"He had some advice on how to deal with the Vietnam issue and the Swift Boat allegations . . ." (the GOP garbage that Kerry hyped his Vietnam record) and he "said these guys play tough and we have to put the Vietnam experience into context and have Kerry talk about it more."

That's it, Joe? You chatted about campaign advice?

Yup.

But, Joe . . . didn't you even ask Burkett about his memos discrediting Bush—the ones Mapes told you about?

Nope.

You're kidding! Nothing but small talk about the Kerry campaign? Yada yada? Then why the hell did you call this guy?

Let me abandon the fanciful dialogue and relay what Joe Lockhart actually told a journalist who asked that very same question. He said:

"I called *you*, didn't I?"

Thanks for the smart-ass answer, Joe. Doesn't matter. No one believes you anyway. You were Kerry's campaign adviser and therefore dedicated—mind, heart, and soul—to seeking any advantage that could swing the election to your boy. Yet you ask enquiring minds to believe that when you phoned an ex-Texas National Guard officer, after being told he had memos discrediting George Bush, and you never even *asked* about them?

With respect, answer the question!

And what does Mary Mapes have to say in her defense? As this is written, CBS says Ms. Mapes has—surprise, surprise!—no comment.

As stated earlier, reporters take great pains to curry favor with sources that dangle blockbuster information. That's fine, up to a point. Rule of thumb, as always, lies in judgment and simple common sense. If they want your wristwatch, what the hell; if they want your first-born, kick 'em in the crotch. Be careful and be advised:

Never do anything that will compromise you as a reporter.

Mapes did. Period. And it wasn't her first tap-dance along the ethical tightrope. Associated Press called her a "talented and dogged reporter," but as an editor who runs reporters, I'd call her an idiot who endangered news operations with her irresponsible behavior. Those are harsh words, but they're what came to mind when I perused a fine piece of reportage by Fox News that dug up a letter to Mapes from the warden of a high-security federal prison in Colorado. In it, he reprimanded her for violating federal regulations and informed her that her press privileges to visit or phone inmates for interviews had been revoked. The warden charged that Mapes—who'd been interviewing a convicted white supremacist—had agreed to the prisoner's illegal request to remail letters he'd send to CBS to an inmate at another prison, thereby keeping "a lot of people out of the loop," as he put it. Said the warden: "The rationale for these restrictions is fairly obvious."

Obvious, indeed. Prison officials monitor mail sent from one convict to another to prevent the hatching of criminal schemes. The warden charged that Mapes had agreed to a mail scam that was illegal and dangerous. With her as unwitting go-between, for example, one convict could send another a CBS-dispatched letter along the lines of:

Dear Spike,

Please do me the favor of offing Prisoner #xxxx, who is currently confined at your joint. Have a nice day and . . . thanks.

Your pal,

Carmine

The warden warned Ms. Mapes that if she persisted in attempting to play post office with his cons, he would take additional steps, such as "referring your actions to the appropriate law enforcement authorities."

Quiz question: What do you get when you rub two wackos together? A firestorm! Burkett and Mapes, busily grinding their own axes, finally wielded them to devastating effect. In one deadly stroke, a legendary news empire was cut to the quick by a phony story—and startling new evidence surfaced indicating that Dan Rather really might be rather biased: His own producer had slipped a CBS scoop to George Bush's Democrat opponents.

Pow! Take that, Daddy and Junior Bush. Bar The Dan from White House interviews, will ya? *Gotcha!*

The *New York Post* summed it up neatly, as they often do, with the headline: "CBS 'Hoaxer' Broker! . . . Producer Probed in Dem Dealings."

Poor Mapes. One couldn't help but feel a bit sorry for her when her long-estranged father suddenly emerged on a Seattle radio talk show and kicked his daughter when she was down:

"I'm really ashamed of my daughter, what she's become," said Don Mapes, who had a falling-out with her years ago for reasons unknown. "She went into journalism with an ax to grind; that is, to promote feminism—and radical feminism, I might say—and liberalism."

Ah, family. Always there when you need them.

Ironically, that somehow got dad and daughter talking again, according to the *New York Daily News*. Mr. Mapes, who's seventy-six, told the paper he'd e-mailed her and warned: "You protect yourself . . . because Dan Rather's not going to do anything but protect himself. She answered back: No way. She said Dan is loyal to me and my bosses are also."

That isn't quite the way Dan assessed the situation after Rathergate, when WCBS-TV asked him if heads would roll. "That I don't know," he said. "But that's not a judgment for me to make."

Courage, Mapes.

Years ago, in a short-lived effort to lighten up Rather's darkish image, CBS yoked him with perky Connie Chung, who asked Walter Cronkite his opinion of the idea. Recalled Connie: "Walter Cronkite sang me a little sea chantey. The verse ended: 'Just watch your back with Dan Rather, dear . . .

Just watch your back with Dan.'"

The "Dannie & Connie" team-up crashed and burned badly. The stiff, awkward anchorman hated management's bid to create a faux "Katie & Matt" ethos, as was documented in *Bias*, the book written by Bernie Goldberg, the ex-CBS news correspondent. He describes in excruciating detail how Rather sabotaged Chung behind her back from within and without, phoning the press and knifing his co-anchor with quotes from "an anonymous network source."

"Just watch your back with Dan, dear. . . ."

Dark thoughts swirl as the Court appraises the landscape of this mythic tale of an oracle suddenly brought down by . . . what?

Hubris.

Isn't that where this story began? And in the mythology man creates to explain his world, isn't this where it always ends? As this is written and we await the independent panel's final verdict, one wonders if they'll report the discovery of the Gollum that surfaced in our earlier tales of Media Elite madness.

Fear.

Will the panel find that fear spawned Rathergate—just as it did at the *Washington Post, USA Today,* the *New York Times,* and all the other newsrooms? Was power wielded with a heavy hand, inspiring such fear of reprisal that otherwise intelligent professionals abandoned their standards and retreated into survival mode?

And speaking of Walter Cronkite, power, and Dan Rather . . . in the Court's never-ending effort to assemble facts some might have missed, let the record show that Fox News reporter Roger

Friedman wrote a relevant and illuminating piece that began so softly one didn't detect the lurking depth-charge until it suddenly went off with an ear-splitting "Aha!"

Two weeks after Rathergate, Friedman was covering a New York show biz bash and ran into Mike Wallace, the veteran star of *60 Minutes*—the Sunday night one, not *60 Minutes* Junior, where the mischief occurred. Friedman asked the grizzled veteran to confirm the "long-running rumor/open secret" that Dan had rather ruthlessly blocked Walter Cronkite from appearing on CBS News since he retired in 1981. For those who may not have noted it—after all, Cronkite has popped up on CBS's David Letterman, syndicated news shows, CNN, cable, etc.—he was banished from making so much as a guest appearance on the Evening News. In nineteen years, he has never, ever been asked back to the newscast he built into a legend. Why not? He was a mere sixty-four when he retired. Rather's seventy-three, but Dan will get work as a correspondent. Why not Walter?

Mike Wallace hunched his shoulders as Friedman asked the question directly: Was this because of Dan Rather's insecurity? Here's Wallace's final answer:

"You said it. And stupidity."

Short and sweet, like bombshells always are.

The media world walks on eggshells as it awaits the verdict that boss of all bosses Sumner Redstone—owner of Viacom, the CBS parent—had promised in a couple of weeks. At this writing, it's been three months. The report by the independent panel might be tough, or it might be a whitewash. But there's no question its very existence scared Rather into the sudden

decision to vacate his anchor chair. Despite years of unques-
tioned power, uneasy lies the head that wore the crown. Hardly
an eye-blink after CBS announced that Dick Thornburgh, a
former attorney general, and Louis D. Boccardi, an ex-execu-
tive of the Associated Press, would investigate the network's
journalistic Krakatoa, Dan Rather leaped right out of his skin.
That was quickly noted in the *New York Times:*

> While the network characterized the two men as constituting
> an independent panel, Mr. Thornburgh's appointment upset
> Dan Rather . . . according to four colleagues and associates,
> Mr. Rather considers Mr. Thornburg a confounding choice in
> part because he served two Republican presidents, Mr. Bush's
> father and Richard M. Nixon, with whom Mr. Rather publicly
> clashed, the colleagues and associates said.

So . . . let's be sure we understand: Dan thinks Republicans
are biased?

As I write this, a December 6 piece on the impending
release of the CBS panel's report by *USA Today* media writer
Peter Johnson includes this quote from our favorite *60
Minutes* loudmouth, Andy Rooney: "There's this ominous
sense of change for the worse, of impending doom."

Ya gotta love Andy, the only guy at CBS who's got the
stones to speak what he sees as the truth of it all—and here it
is, as told to a rapt audience at Tufts University: "I am very
critical of some of the people at CBS who make it apparent
what their political leanings are. That's what happened to this

thing of Dan Rather's that got out. There's no question they wanted to run it because it was negative towards Bush."

Who do you suppose he means by "they"?

If there's anyone who should survive this CBS mess, it's Andy Rooney—the cranky old bastard. He's probably the only newsperson Ed Murrow's ghost is still talking to!

Chapter 11

Back to September 8. CBS executives would later admit that the editorial process on this Wednesday edition of *60 Minutes* had moved "faster than usual." And now it was the moment of truth . . . or rather, untruth. Executive Producer Josh Howard pulled the trigger.

Dan Rather peered out at the nation, intense as usual, looking like this might be the night he'd announce that CBS had captured the aliens and we were "going live to the hangar where they're secretly being held!" Solemnly, the man the White House loves to hate announced that CBS had acquired secret documents that would expose George Bush, once and for all, as a military malingerer!

The die was cast. Dan had dropped the bomb—and the fallout is still raining down. Within hours, the so-called "bloggers in pajamas" were ripping the documents as fake. Then the Establishment Press charged in, aggressively questioning the memos. CBS stiff-armed them all. By Friday, September 10, the firestorm was raging. Dan Rather huffed: "CBS News stands by, and I stand by, the thoroughness and accuracy of this report, period."

Period.

In Danish, that rather scary language Bernie Goldberg taught us, "period" means *"Shut up!"*

On Sunday, September 12, embattled CBS News President Andrew Heyman—either not sure what the hell had happened or perfectly willing to lie about it—swore like a good network soldier: "The story was thoroughly vetted, as all pieces of *60 Minutes* are. . . . We used every appropriate journalistic standard and safeguard in reporting the story."

And how did Andrew Heyward get to be president of CBS News? He once was Dan Rather's TV producer. Heyward's the guy who let Dan walk off the set and leave his network dark for six long minutes.

On Monday, September 13, Rather assured America: "CBS used several techniques to make sure these papers should be taken seriously."

Seriously? You hear them screams from the White House, hoss? They're takin' it more seriously than a whore who gets paid with a check!

Rather kept ranting, in trademark turgid prose, that it was only "partisan political ideological forces" that were attacking the story. His theory took a Texas ass-whuppin' on Tuesday, September 14. Rival network ABC interviewed two CBS experts, and they flat-out punched an ice pick in Dan's tire! They insisted they'd warned CBS the documents could be forgeries but were ignored. Hot on the heels of that shocker, spunky CBS spokesgal Sandy Genelius bounced into the spotlight, chirping cheery assurance that the network was "confident about the chain of custody. We're confident in how we secured the documents."

New York Post columnist Maggie Gallagher dipped her pen in poison and wrote about one of Dan's astounding pronouncements in the *New York Observer*, to wit: *"I know this story is true."*

Here is Gallagher's take, perfectly put:

"I know this story is true." When I heard Dan Rather say this on the Friday after the story broke, I said to myself, "Something really weird is going on here." Journalists don't talk like that. How could Dan *know* this story was true? Was he there? Did he see it personally? Of course not. Why was he vouching for the story in the language of faith, not like a hard-headed journalist reporting the evidence? Explain to us, Dan, why CBS News as an organization echoed this faith-based reporting at the highest levels, flipping the burden of proof and attacking critics' motives in a way that struck most journalists (not just me or Rush Limbaugh) . . . as really odd.

Gallagher then raised a point touched on earlier in our Trial of Dan Rather—if you're going to get experts, get the best. The *National Enquirer* uses FBI-trained experts, among others, and—unlike CBS News—we thoroughly check them out. It's not a difficult exercise for print journalists. When *USA Today* sniffed the stink rising off Dan's documents, it took them less that a day to find two FBI-trained experts who labeled them forgeries.

Despite his own experts back-pedaling away from the memos, Dan just hunkered in the bunker, not even acting particularly defensive. Indeed, he accused journalists of focusing on the forgeries and, as he put it, "ignoring the larger story." After all, Dan Rather "knows" it's true, so why back it up with solid facts and documents that are not forged? You, the Jury, should consider the following evidence of unbridled arrogance in your final deliberations, to wit: even after the CBS mess had exploded like a drowned hog after a week in a creek, Dan declared, in a *Chicago Tribune* interview, that he *still* didn't think his Bush-bashing memos were forgeries!

So why, the Court inquires, did you and CBS apologize, Mr. Rather? Why, on Monday, September 20, did the network belatedly state officially that "CBS News cannot prove that the documents are authentic, which is the only acceptable journalistic standard to justify using them in the report? We should not have used them. That was a mistake, which we deeply regret."

Apparently, you now disagree with CBS and your statement, sir. Two days after the admission of irresponsibility, you told the *Chicago Tribune* that you refute the charge that documents used to smear a sitting president were *not* forged, in your opinion. The Court finds this a puzzling reversal. You are backing off from the original statement you made, which was, in part: "We have been misled on the key question of how our source for the documents came into possession of these papers. . . . We made a mistake in judgment, and for that I am sorry."

"We have been misled. . . ."

Hmm. The Court finds that equivocating phrase vaguely familiar. No matter . . . it may come to us later . . . but right now, we hear from celebrated expert Ken Auletta, a media critic who often writes of these things in *New Yorker* magazine. In a PBS television interview, Auletta took issue with the fact that the Fox News Channel "treated this story as if it were Watergate. It's not Watergate."

Ah, Watergate . . . of course! That's where we first heard the phrase, "We have been misled." It all makes sense now, this feeling of *déjà vu*. Secret documents . . . sending secret operatives on behind-the-scenes political missions . . . dirty tricks . . . stonewalling . . . paranoia about the press . . . resignation under fire . . . and that weaselish phrase, "We have been misled." How ironic that Dan Rather is finally possessed by the spirit of Richard Nixon, his first Republican nemesis, Tricky Dick.

To put it another way, not very originally, *In the end, Dan became Richard Nixon.*

In the Court's view, Rathergate is the journalistic equivalent of Watergate. It's a question that will be argued forever in the press, in journalism schools and in bars where journalists gather to lift a jar. Some defend Dan Rather; some believe history will treat him harshly. There are many journalists who have castigated him, so let us quote some defenders. Tom Shales, the *Washington Post* TV critic who amusingly dubbed Rather "Gunga Dan" years ago, rationalized that Rather stonewalled to the bitter end because "he is a team player, and he wanted to support the team." Shales added that he "tried to defend the group behind him. So you can hardly blame him for that."

Even if that were true, blind loyalty is no defense for fraud. The Court does not agree that journalism is akin to *Monday Night Football*. You do not support the "team" when it produces false reports. And we certainly can "blame" a journalist who tries to "defend" colleagues who've produced lies that could have been avoided if professional standards had been followed.

Remember: Always think of the reader.

And who says the team "behind him" was at fault? Did fear of thwarting a bit-in-his-mouth boss render reporters into unwilling straw men for slovenly journalism? Only the report will tell us.

Weighing in as a Dan Fan, David Bianculli writes in the *New York Daily News:* "Rather ought to be judged less for the use of questionable documents than for how he and CBS corrected the process that let them slip through, and for what he says and does next."

The Court is stunned. Does Bianculli know something that we do not? He states that Rather and CBS should be judged for how they "corrected the process that let them slip through." The word "corrected" is past tense. As of this writing, *nothing* has been corrected. As this book goes to press, there is no report from the independent panel . . . no announcement of changes in standard operating procedure . . . no explanation of how the mess occurred . . . no word on the weeding out of incompetent staffers, if there are any. How does that add up to CBS correcting anything?

Ironically, right next to Bianculli's column is a box headlined, "A Tale of Woe." It shows how Dan Rather's statements gradually changed from saying that the documents "were provided by unimpeachable sources," (September 10) to "I no longer have confidence in these documents" (September 20).

The Court repeats that shortly after his "no confidence" statement, Rather told the *Chicago Tribune* that he "still" does not believe they are forgeries. Sound familiar?

"I am not a crook."

The Court is confused because Rather confuses the issue. Was his apology sincere? Or does he intend to spend the rest of his days hinting that he actually did broadcast a really solid story—no matter what you heard, podnuh! It will be crucial, as Bianculli says, to see "what he will do and say next."

Another Dan Rather ally when the CBS firestorm broke out was retiring NBC News anchorman Tom Brokaw, who defended his rival against charges that he used forged documents to attack the president. He lashed out at critics of the CBS anchor in October, saying that they had waged "a kind of political jihad against Dan Rather and CBS News that is quite outrageous."

An amazing statement. It underscores how haircuts who read teleprompters see themselves as a breed apart, who should never be challenged by legitimate questions from other newsmen. Why would Tom Brokaw argue against the press asking tough questions about a major news story that looked questionable?

By November, Brokaw had backed off noticeably. He admitted to *Time* magazine that Rather had made "a very big mistake."

David Broder, respected political correspondent for the *Washington Post*, said that after a half-century in the business of journalism, "I certainly feel a sense of shame and embarrassment at our performance." In citing Rather's story based on a "forged document," Broder believes that "the professional practices and code of responsibility in journalism have suffered a body blow."

In days gone by, he adds, "Any Texan with a grudge against George Bush and the National Guard who suddenly produced a purported photocopy of an explosive thirty-year-old order signed by a dead man would have been treated with the deep distrust he deserved by the reporters to whom he offered his wares. And no professional journalist would have made a call to the Kerry campaign encouraging a flack to contact this dubious source."

In a truly bizarre development, Dan was defended by Fox TV star Bill O'Reilly—a conservative who abhors liberals and has chided Dan for his Dem-loving ways on his no-spin show. Media insiders—and probably many of Bill's fans—were surprised when O'Reilly made a strong and impassioned case for Dan's basic integrity in his newspaper column. O'Reilly went ballistic about how Dan had been "slimed" by the press. He wrote:

> The ordeal of Dan Rather goes far beyond the man himself. It speaks to the presumption of guilt that now rules the day in America. Because of a ruthless and callow media, no citizen, much less one who achieves fame, is given the benefit of the doubt when it comes to allegations or personal attacks. The smearing of America is in full bloom.

Gee, Bill, are you talking about George Bush? He was just attacked and slimed—by Dan Rather. Or are you talking about yourself? You just endured weeks of headlines and cable TV chatter because of charges made by a woman in your employ—not that you mention that in your article, but the adumbration resonates. You're understandably sensitive on this issue, but I know you and your essential fairness. I have to disagree that Dan Rather was slimed. Dan was asked legitimate questions about an explosive story that was rightly discredited because it was based on forged documents and sloppy journalism. The reason it blew up into a huge morality play—and on my celebrity beat, I'm something of an expert in how scandal plays out—is because Dan refused to own up quickly to the problems with the story. If he'd done that swiftly and forthrightly, this brouhaha would have faded fast. Teapot tempests about journalism are *booooring* for the general public—Dan Rather is, after all, no Paris Hilton.

Remember when he got caught fronting a Democratic fundraiser in Texas? Dan quickly went on Geraldo Rivera's show and admitted he been as "dumb as a sack full of hammers" for appearing to be biased for a political party. I've never heard anyone mention this story again . . . unless Rush Limbaugh's still ranting about it.

O'Reilly interviewed Rather on the *O'Reilly Factor* in 2001. When asked if he thought Bill Clinton is an honest man, Rather replied, "I do." O'Reilly followed up by asking, "Even though he lied in [TV journalist] Jim Lehrer's face about the Lewinsky case?" Rather replied: "Who among us has not lied about something?" The following exchange was rather prophetic, as it turns out:

O'REILLY: Well, I didn't lie to anyone's face on national television. I don't think you have. Have you?

RATHER: I don't think I ever have. I hope I never have

Congratulations, Bill. Your interview with a major anchorman was quite revealing. (How about O'Reilly replacing Rather on CBS?) Now, would you like to hear Dan Rather lie on the airwaves?

I'm all news, all the time. Full power, tall tower. I want to break in when the news breaks out. That's my agenda. Now, respectfully, when you start talking about a liberal agenda and all the, quote, "liberal bias" in the media, I quite frankly, and I say this respectfully but candidly to you, I don't know what you're talking about. (To Denver KOA's Mike Rosen, November 28, 1995.)

This from the man who inspired this phrase in a *New York Times* headline: "Fake But True!" Chisel that on your tombstone, CBS.

"Slime" Dan Rather? Journalists like David Broder and Tim Rutten and Andy Rooney and Don Hewitt and Mike Walker have the right to criticize a so-called journalist who declares, in the *New York Observer:* "The longer we go without a denial in such things—this story is true." The utter illogic, the total dumbness of his statement is staggering. By that standard, I could publish in my *National Enquirer* column that Dan Rather's new hobby is juggling live rattlesnakes, and the story would stand as truth unless and until he denies it. Rather exists on another plane, where he invents and reinvents the rules of newsgathering. He has rejected quaint customs practiced by journalists here on Earth.

What's the frequency, Kenneth?

Chapter 12

Hear ye, hear ye! The Trial of Dan Rather now convenes for its final session. It is time to render a verdict and pronounce sentencing. The Court thanks all those who have attended and served on our jury. Hopefully, we have learned some things about journalism, a supposedly high-minded calling that, as we have observed, is quite easily buffeted and corrupted by our human nature.

By attitudes like: *Hubris.*

By emotions like: *Fear.*

The Court notes that we have indulged in a bit of rough frontier fun with that famed son of the Lone Star State, Dan Rather—some of it good-natured, some at his expense. We apologize for whatever seemed mean-spirited, but we remind him of what he told Bernie Goldberg: "This is a vicious and competitive business, and anybody who forgets it does so at his peril."

As the Court convenes for this, its final session, the world still awaits the report on Rathergate by the CBS independent panel. The December 10, 2004, *New York Post* reports that embattled CBS News producer Mary Mapes has written a sixty-eight-page statement in her defense, "lobbying to convince the CBS probers that Rather's exposé on Bush's

National Guard service was accurate, even if the documents obtained from a crackpot Texas Democrat were bogus. Rather acted preemptively by quitting as the 'Evening News' anchor. The big question now is whether CBS News President Andrew Heyward will be forced out."

Astounding. The Court, skeptical by nature, suspects that vicious political infighting is going on behind the closed doors of CBS. One hears vague rumors that some network executives are arguing that only parts of the report should be made public. If true, that would be a public relations disaster that will keep the scandal of Rathergate piping hot for years to come. The Court would remind the jury that the independent report was promised in "a few weeks." It has been three months.

So the Court stands alone and will proceed with its business, beginning with evidence relevant to Dan Rather's rush to judgment of one man's military record on the basis of what he should have known were forged documents. Now it has come to the Court's attention that Dan Rather's own military record has been attacked in a book called *Stolen Valor*, by the author B. G. Burkett—no relation, apparently, to the above-mentioned "crackpot Texas Democrat" Bill Burkett, although the Court cannot warrant that this is so, because the Court intends to treat this evidence the way it should be treated without a full journalistic investigation. In other words, the Court will comment on an existing "document"—the book *Stolen Valor*—but will not make any warranties as to its "authenticity," because the Court has not journalistically investigated the truth of its claims, even though the book has been published and reviewed, and its veracity apparently has never been challenged.

In plain language, I got no reason to disbelieve this dang book, hoss—but I ain't sayin' it's true, neither. I'm jest tryin' to make a point, and here it comes: author B. G. Burkett claims that you, Dan Rather, have greatly exaggerated your own military record. He says that you have claimed you are a United Sates Marine, but you are not.

The book *Stolen Valor* is a history of the media's portrayal of the Vietnam conflict. *NewsMax* magazine reported in 2002 that author B. G. Burkett "says he's tired of Rather's double-talk and hypocrisy." Case in point, he says, is in the book *Bias,* by Bernie Goldberg, which came under examination by the Court in earlier sessions. The jury will remember well Goldberg's dramatic confrontation with a very angry Dan Rather, who was furious about Goldberg's *Wall Street Journal* article about liberal bias in the media.

"Angry I was expecting," Goldberg told *Bias* readers. "What came next, I wasn't. Rather's voice started quivering, and he told me how in his young days, he had signed up with the Marines—not once, but twice!"

According to the *NewsMax* report: "This is not the first time Rather has hid behind the flag and his own military service claims to deflect criticism of his reporting, Burkett said. He is flabbergasted that Rather continues to proudly describe himself as a 'Marine.'" Burkett explains that Rather "signed up for the military twice, not the Marines," and that he "never got through Marine recruit training because he couldn't do the physical activity … [and] was discharged less than four months later on May 11, 1954, for being medically unfit." It is known that Dan Rather suffered from rheumatic fever as a child.

As for Rather's alleged claim to Bernie Goldberg that he signed up for the Marines twice, Burkett—who avers that he researched Rather's military records—says Rather signed up for the Army Reserves once when he attended Sam Houston University, but later dropped out, then graduated and signed up for the Marines.

"So he signed up for the Marine Corps once," Burkett is quoted by NewsMax. "He's made such a big deal of this 'I'm a Marine' thing . . . [but] you're not a real Marine until you get out of basic training. And he never got out of basic training. . . . This is like a guy who flunks out of Harvard running around saying he went to Harvard."

So, Rather quit once, washed out once. That means he's neither an ex-soldier nor an ex-Marine, according to B. G. Burkett.

Once again, the Court has no reason to disbelieve any of the above about Rather's military record. The Court could quite easily check military archives. It would be my first move if I had the least interest in proving or disproving these allegations. But I do . . . not . . . give . . . a . . . damn. The Court has brought this evidence to the jury's attention because it is sobering to realize that, when all is said and done, this flag-waving anchorman unfairly attacked a man who served his country. George W. Bush joined the Texas National Guard, completed basic training and qualified as a pilot of military jet planes. He was honorably discharged. As an honorably discharged member of the U.S. Air Force (four years active duty stateside and with Fifth Air Force in the Far East), I can tell you that making the cut as a flying officer is no small thing.

Even if Dan Rather's phony memos *were* true—so what?

The worst Bush would be guilty of is what we G.I.s used to call "flubbing the dub"—making sure we didn't work too damn hard! If you'd ever been a G.I., Dan, you'd understand the term. And now that we're down to it, according to B. G. Burkett, the only reason that you joined the Army Reserve in college was to duck the Korean War draft. True or not true?

With respect, answer the question.

And don't hesitate to answer, because my point here is—even if you *were* trying to stay one step ahead of the draft, I repeat . . . so what? Most guys will try to slide around a military obligation if they've got something going on, like college. Bill Clinton did. It's not against the law, for Pete's sake!

That's why it surprises me that a guy like you—who's been ridiculed in the public prints as a *faux* Marine by B. G. Burkett—wouldn't feel just a bit ashamed about sliming a president's military record. And if you truly believed you needed to expose him, you should have made damn sure you did your job as a journalist.

You should have gotten it right, Dan.

And just for the record, as anyone who knows me will attest, I have no political affiliation. I am certainly no fan of President Bush. I've broadcast that fact loud and long on my radio show and in my weekly appearances on Howard Stern's show. I am a newspaperman, pal, and proud to be an equal opportunity basher. And if there's anyone who needs bashing right now, it's you.

Please rise and hear this Court's verdict.

Guilty: Of getting suckered by a story that wouldn't fool a high school journalist.

Guilty: Of leading your team into disaster, then leaving them to twist in the wind.

Guilty: Of lying to the end, even when you *knew* you'd gone wrong—leaving your audience to twist in the wind.

Guilty: Of smearing fellow journalists who asked legitimate questions about your story, calling them—and those proud pajama-clad bloggers—partisan ideologues.

The Court dismisses for lack of sufficient evidence the charges of political bias and of knowingly allowing Mary Mapes to aid the Kerry campaign.

The Court finds that you should have been reprimanded and fired from CBS News. To your defense attorneys—Barbara Walters, Peter Jennings, et al.—the Court rejects the eloquent pleadings that you should be forgiven because you have made just one mistake of this magnitude in your long career. That is an argument often heard in courts. A quick, somewhat over-the-top way to understand why it is not compelling is to apply it to the case of, say, a Scott Peterson or O.J. Simpson.

Sometimes, "magnitude" *is* the point.

Even if Scott Peterson had been the world's greatest husband, all his good deeds would have been negated by his final transgression. Peterson and Simpson were not, of course, perfect husbands. And you were not the perfect reporter. Some acts are too harmful to go unpunished. In the end, it was not that you got it wrong—it was that you still refuse to accept that you did.

The ghost of Edward R. Murrow agrees. You disgraced yourself and the proud news tradition of CBS.

Tiffany schmiffany, right?

Courage, Dan.